Praise for *People Matter at Work*

"Culture can be a buzzword—until you read this book. Josh brings culture to life in a way that is actionable, authentic, and full of hope. *People Matter at Work* offers a clear path to building a workplace where people are seen, supported, and invited to bring their best. Every leader and leader wannabe should read this."

—Keith Granger, president and CEO of Granger Waste Services

"In *People Matter at Work*, Josh gives a fresh perspective on the recommended focuses of any business leader: trust and empathy. Josh's leadership journey is what I appreciated most in *People Matter at Work*. Most desire leadership roles, but opportunities to lead never arrive according to our schedule. Hearing Josh's story will inspire others to take that chance and be better prepared for when that opportunity presents itself. This book matches the needs for both established and aspiring leaders."

—Gonzalo Alberto Diaz, CEO of Centella

"*People Matter at Work* truly resonates with my values and reminds me why I love my job. As a leader, you must truly care, inspire others, and grow alongside your team. This book is not just another leadership guide—it's Josh's honest, very personal story and a refreshing, hands-on invitation to reflect, learn, and stay focused on the people behind performance, genuine team spirit, and the passion to make a difference together."

—Christiane Bernhardt, president of customer services at Siemens Healthineers

"In today's business world, it's easy to forget that behind every success story are real people. At Block Imaging, that truth is at the heart of everything—and *People Matter at Work* brings it to life. Told through the inspiring story of an extraordinary leader, this book celebrates the infinite value and dignity of every team member. Josh's leadership is more than a philosophy—it's a way of life. With humility, determination, and contagious energy, Josh and his team have built a thriving, profitable company while never losing sight of what matters most: people.

"For any leader longing to build a culture of genuine care in an age of burnout, cynicism, and cutthroat competition, *People Matter at Work* offers both inspiration and proof that leading with the heart is not only possible—it's powerful."

—Anita Philip, senior HR professional with International Justice Mission

"G. K. Chesterton once wrote, 'It is always the secure who are humble.' Josh's humility has led to an honest expression of a confidence-inspiring leadership with his sincere actions. In *People Matter at Work*, he now does the same with his sincere words."

—Dr. Marv Tazelaar, founder of American MRI

"In *People Matter at Work*, Josh shares personal stories, honest lessons, and powerful reminders that leadership isn't about titles or formulas—it's about character, trust, and truly valuing people. What makes this book so refreshing is that Josh doesn't pretend to have all the answers. Instead, he invites us into his journey and reflects on the learning, growth, and even the stumbles that helped shape a people-first culture. It's an inspiring and practical read that will challenge you to rethink *how* you connect with others and *what* it means to lead well."

—Jason Newmark, executive director of AHRA

"*People Matter at Work* provides a simple yet powerful road map I have been able to use in my roles since seeing it lived out in Josh's day-to-day leadership. The 'Me' vs 'We' cycles are game-changing, and I know this will be the next book I ask all our leaders to read."

—Bill Clark, president of Baxter Enterprises

"Josh Block has given us more than a leadership book; he has written a practical guide for building organizational cultures where people are the ultimate focus. With vulnerability and honesty, he writes as a practitioner who has mastered these lessons and is now ready to teach us. His stories provide achievable steps and compelling arguments, offering guidance for leaders at any stage of their journey. *People Matter at Work* is a timely and necessary companion for anyone who longs to lead with integrity and impact. By focusing on people first, Josh helps us see that collective work in community is not only possible but essential for flourishing organizations. I recommend this book wholeheartedly."

—D. Michael Lindsay, PhD, president of Taylor University

"Josh Block's *People Matter at Work* isn't just theory; it's tested truth. He reveals how leadership isn't about control or charisma but consistency. Repeatedly treating people as if they matter is what sets the best leaders apart. His lived experience proves that when people thrive, performance follows. Real, relatable, and deeply human."

—Preston Poore, author of *How Is Greater Than What: Master the Growth and Leadership Skill Everyone Else Ignores*, speaker, trainer, and coach

People Matter @work

JOSH BLOCK

Forefront
BOOKS

People Matter at Work: Fostering a Culture Where Team Members Thrive and Everyone Wins
Copyright © 2026 by Josh Block

All rights reserved. No part of this publication may be reproduced, stored in a retrieval system, or transmitted in any form by any means, electronic, mechanical, photocopy, recording, or otherwise, without the prior permission of the publisher, except as provided by USA copyright law.

No patent liability is assumed with respect to the use of the information contained herein. Although every precaution has been taken in the prepar ation of this book, the publisher and author assume no responsibility for errors or omissions. Neither is any liability assumed for damages resulting from the use of the information contained herein.

Published by Forefront Books, Nashville, Tennessee.
Distributed by Simon & Schuster.

Library of Congress Control Number: 2025924485

Print ISBN: 978-1-63763-504-9
E-book ISBN: 978-1-63763-505-6

Cover Design by Studio Gearbox
Interior Design by PerfecType, Nashville, TN

Printed in the United States of America
26 27 28 29 30 31 RR4 10 9 8 7 6 5 4 3 2 1

Contents

Foreword by Krista Kotrla	7
Preface	13
Acknowledgments	19
Introduction	27

PART I
Tripping into Leadership   35

Chapter 1: Sales Rep to President	37
Chapter 2: The Me-Cycle and the Gift of Humble Pie	63
Chapter 3: Revealing the Heart of Culture	83

PART II
The Three T's   105

Chapter 4: Better *Together*	111
Chapter 5: The Power of *Thoughtful* Decisions	135
Chapter 6: Open the Window to *Transparency*	165

CONTENTS

PART III
The We-Cycle at Work   191

Chapter 7: The Three S's	193
Chapter 8: *Trust*	205
Chapter 9: *Ownership* and *Generosity*	217
Conclusion	235
Further Reading	239

Foreword by Krista Kotrla

> In order to build a culture of trust, you have to move from separation to a connection worldview. When the worldview is right, a person is able to lead, innovate, and create from a position of authenticity and freedom.
>
> —Jamie Winship

I've known Josh Block for more than two decades. We first met as peers, and I later had the privilege of reporting to him for six years. Since my departure from Block Imaging, we've taken turns advising each other, driven by a shared passion for and pursuit of building healthy, people-first work cultures. Josh leads. I consult. And through it all, we've remained friends. That friendship has been marked by his unwavering encouragement—even when it cost him something. When I felt like I'd failed onstage in front of the entire company, Josh quietly pulled me aside and said, "I'm proud of you." Not because he couldn't and wouldn't tell me the kind truth about my delivery but because in that moment, what I needed most wasn't critique. It was belief. The tools for success could come later.

When I told Josh another company had created a COO role near my home in Dallas that felt tailor-made for my wiring, his immediate response was "You should take it!" He wasn't thinking about what was best for him or even the company he was leading. He was thinking about what was best for me and my family. That's who he is.

Years later, when I was offered what was, in many ways, a dream consulting opportunity—with one of his own heroes, no less—Josh didn't flinch. He celebrated with me and championed the opportunity for me to grow.

In each of these moments and countless others, his leadership has always flowed from an uncommon belief in people and view of work.

And that's what makes this book so important.

At the heart of leadership are two divergent worldviews. One is built on *separation*. The other is built on *connection*.[1]

---

[1] Jamie and Donna Winship, *Identity Method Masterclass* (online course), 2025, https://www.identityexchange.com/identitymethod.

Leaders with a *separation worldview* see the world through the lens of "us versus them" and create cultures fraught with scarcity, blame, fear, detachment, and self-protection. They lead from a need for control. They guard their own credibility. They see relationships as transactional. Their cultures are **high on pressure** and **low on trust**. They may achieve results, but often at the cost of their own people.

Leaders who adopt a *connection worldview*, on the other hand, galvanize people to move together and foster cultures filled with growth, grace, curiosity, trust, and interdependence. They believe people are inherently valuable—not just useful. They take the long view. They don't fear mistakes; they learn from them. Their cultures are marked by clarity, safety, and shared ownership. And as a result, their people and their organizations flourish.

Josh leads from a **connection worldview**.

He believes deeply and consistently that people matter. Because of that, he leads, innovates, and creates from a place of authenticity and freedom. And as it turns out, that kind of leadership not only produces healthier people, but it also drives better outcomes.

If you're already a connection-oriented leader, Josh's journey and the "We-Cycle" will affirm and sharpen your convictions. It will give you language for what you've sensed and likely save you years of trial and error.

If you lead from a separation mindset, I have good news and bad news.

The bad news? Josh's decisions, stories, and leadership style might feel confusing or perhaps even frustrating.

The good news? Paradigms can shift. Stories can change people. And if you're willing, this book might just reshape how you lead and see the people you're entrusted with.

As an organizational health consultant with the Table Group, a Patrick Lencioni company, I witness every day how deeply leaders impact teams, cultures, communities, and ultimately, the lives of hundreds—sometimes thousands—of families across generations.

Leadership is high-stakes work.

Now imagine being thrust into that responsibility unexpectedly. You're in your twenties. The company is in crisis mode. Your older siblings now report to you. Employees' families are watching closely. Vendors are unsure you can carry the weight. The team is asking, "Are you ready for this?"

That's the moment Josh stepped into.

It's no surprise, then, that he's written this book not just to reflect on what happened but to share the beliefs and practices that helped make Block Imaging not only successful but a place where people thrive.

That's what makes *People Matter at Work* so powerful.

Josh charts a path. He shares real stories, tough decisions, and hard-won insights that bring the We-Cycle to life. Not just the *how* of healthy leadership but the *why* that sustains it.

And while the frameworks and takeaways are practical across industries and roles, don't miss the deeper invitation beneath it all:

You matter.

Preface

There's no shortage of how-to books that attempt to reverse engineer modern leadership. Many writers have sought to boil down the unique attributes of successful people, believing that if we can replicate their actions, attitudes, or behaviors, we'll somehow duplicate their outsized results in our own stories. We analyze everyone from Nelson Mandela to Mother Teresa, Southwest Airlines to Chick-fil-A, the UConn Lady Huskies to the Kansas City Chiefs. Deep down, we hope that if we mimic their diets, exercise routines, sleep habits, or communication styles, we'll enjoy the same success they've achieved.

For every book that zeroes in on *humility* as the common thread among successful leaders—and there are plenty—there's a podcast that points to *execution* as the key differentiator. (After all, everything depends on a leader's ability to execute, right?) Or is *discipline* the secret ingredient: a daily routine that begins before sunrise, avoids ineffective meetings, and prescribes reading a book a week? Is that the ticket to leadership success? Maybe it's learning to *embrace failure*, because if you're not failing, you're not taking big enough risks . . . right?

Maybe the answer is better found in a symphony of qualities that flow from who we are and what we believe about people and leadership as a whole? Don't get me wrong, humility is essential for any healthy leader, and we'll explore it further in a bit, but nobody wants to follow a humble leader with terrible instincts. Or how about the leader with off-the-charts discipline but who lacks proper balance or the flexibility to change course when needed? Or the one who executes like a boss but never gets buy-in from their team? As the saying goes, "A leader without followers is just a man or a woman out for a walk." Or how about the elevation of risk-taking? There's no question that it's an essential element of good leadership, but it's celebrated only when it works, right? After all, who wants to put their lives in the hands of a leader who bets the entire organization's future on an idea that fails because of poor timing or insufficient resources?

At the end of the day, the right book at the right time has been transformational in my life and leadership, especially when I sought to find my footing after transitioning from a regional sales rep to company president over the course of a weekend in 2011. That's where this book begins. No matter how lost or ill-equipped you might feel right now, you'd be hard-pressed to find someone less ready to be thrust into leadership than I was at twenty-nine years old.

Since that wild weekend, it's been a gift to stand on the shoulders of leaders further down the path as our family business expanded from a team of fifty to more than four hundred, while annual revenues of Block Imaging grew from $30 million to more than $200 million. I'm so grateful to Jim Collins, Brené Brown, Patrick Lencioni, and countless others for their wisdom. Collins's "Bullets Before Cannonballs," Brown's "Clear Is Kind," and Lencioni's *The Advantage* are central to the Block University course that every new team member attends. The principles and stories shared in books like *The Founder's Mentality*, *The Power of Moments*, *Grit*, *Everybody Matters*, *Extreme Ownership*, *The Leadership Challenge*, and hundreds of others have poured fuel on the fire as we've sought to create a place where people love to work.

Having led and observed countless leaders inside and outside of our organization, **I'm convinced that strong leadership is not primarily a function of positional authority or of one specific trait but is born out of deep trust and authentic character that can only flow from true relationship.** In short, the best leaders treat people like they matter. Over and over. Even when it's hard, takes a little longer, and costs us something. People are hungry to follow leaders who look beyond their own desires and invite them into becoming more than they'd ever dreamed of and into a mission worth investing in. They're desperate to work with leaders who protect, prioritize, and promote the growth and well-being of the people they lead. Put simply, they want to work for people who embody "we" over "me." Bosses who focus primarily on "getting what they want" may have *employees* (a word you won't hear me use often) who show up with their bodies and minds but who leave their hearts at home. Ugh.

Words like *culture* and *leadership* have been overused, oversimplified, glorified, questioned, and rightly criticized. If *leadership* and *culture* feel too abstract (or if ropes courses and trust falls are all that come to mind), bear with me. I'm just as apprehensive about writing a book on culture and leadership as you are about reading another one. What if it gets 1.9 stars on Amazon, like James Patterson's *You've Been Warned*?

All joking aside, regardless of where you are on your leadership journey, **this book is written for you *and* for the people you lead** (or will lead someday). I hope *People Matter at Work* will inspire, equip, and empower you to foster a vibrant, deeply engaged, high-trust, and high-performance culture. While this type of leader is far too rare, the culture they create is the foundation of healthy organizations, strong businesses, flourishing families, and championship teams.

Our roles and industries may look different, and every leadership story is unique, but some principles and lessons transcend context. They were all hard-earned and are as important for me as a leader and our organization today as they were when we first stumbled across them. Teddy Roosevelt was spot-on when he said, **"Leadership is full of dust, sweat, and blood."**

So cheers to you for stepping into the leadership arena. I'm grateful for you, and I consider it a privilege to champion the leader you're becoming and the culture you're creating. Thank you for leading and for your willingness to walk this journey together. "Let's roll."[2]

Josh Block
Lansing, Michigan, 2026

---

[2] Todd Beamer's final words aboard United Flight 93 on September 11th, 2001. Two words that embodied true courage and became a rallying cry for a nation.

Acknowledgments

This book was written on the shoulders of so many who both poured into and believed in me as a person and a leader—long before I knew what was possible myself. While most acknowledgment sections are tucked into the back, it's an honor to appreciate those who've so indelibly shaped and supported my life and leadership as the foundation for *People Matter at Work*:

Lacey, your leadership in my life is incomparable. It's a high privilege to be your husband. You have simultaneously sharpened, encouraged, and softened me over the last twenty-six years. You are my life editor, protecting and inviting me into growing in my areas of weakness and just flat-out making me a better leader every day.

Anneliese and Jamin, I'm so thankful for your endless affection and grace as I practice being a dad to you two. Thanks for sharing your daddy with the Block Imaging team over all these years. I'm so proud of and thankful for both of you and can't wait to watch your stories unfold as Mom and I launch you into the world.

Dad, for teaching the value of hard work and the power of business from the start. Your decision to take a risk and found Block Imaging in 1997 has impacted so many . . . and the story's just beginning. Your belief and willingness to entrust this team and the car keys to the next generation is so deeply respected and appreciated.

Mom, you are the epitome of faith. You embody and model the three T's as well as any leader I've ever seen. Your unending love and care for the needs of others is second to none. It's been said that children gravitate toward the oldest person who takes them seriously. The fact that you are surrounded by young people is a great testament to the potential you see in everyone.

Tony and Barb, thank you for cheering us on, supporting us every step of the way, and loving our kids like nobody else.

The Block Imaging Team, the way you embody our mission and work together to serve one another and the healthcare community is exemplary. What a privilege it's been to hire and work alongside each of you in writing an uncommon story together. Thank you for continuing to build an organization we want our kids to work for someday!

The Block Imaging Leadership Team, there are no words to describe my gratitude. Your vision, ambition, and passion for people is remarkable. Thank you for chasing after the mission and for serving this team for more than 120 years between the eight of us!

ACKNOWLEDGMENTS

Jason Crawford, side by side. That's how we've walked, and what a gift it's been. You carry a rare blend of steady presence and relentless optimism that's so unwavering it invites a double take. And yet, after all these years, I can say with full confidence, it's not a performance: It's who you are. Whether it's solving problems, coaching team members, or just grabbing coffee with someone who needs a lift, you do it with sincerity, joy, and full presence. You've modeled what it means to be mission-minded and people-first without compromising either, and that has left a lasting mark on this organization and on me personally. You're the kind of leader who multiplies belief, who reminds people what's possible, and who lives with an abundance mentality like none other. I can't wait to read *your* book someday—the one that unpacks what it's like to live life and lead with that kind of overflow. Thank you for walking this road together. I'm better because of it.

Emily Jones, you are one of the hungriest, most teachable, and grittiest people I've ever met. I couldn't imagine a better executive assistant, trusted sounding board, and friend. Long before you began leading the parts sales team, you were leading with heart, resilience, and a deep care for people. You carry courage in spades and, as Chris Sharrock says it perfectly, "You're like the shoe that fits every occasion." You've been flexible, dependable, and unwaveringly present through every season. And those thousands of yeses—each one a small act of trust and sacrifice—laid the groundwork for the story we're living today. Thank you for believing, for showing up, and for helping carry the vision every step of the way.

Chris and Christine, for the way you two see and believe in me, cover my backside, and call me into my destiny. I'll never forget the day you (Chris) sat in my office and said you wanted to do something big. What a total blast it's been working together over the last twenty years and leading together over the last seven. You're an incredible leader and one of the best followers I've ever led. Climb on, bro. Climb on.

Jason, Jeremy, and Jon, my three brothers—your trust and belief has made this uncommon journey possible. While many families look to a business to mine for treasure, you guys have always viewed it as a garden to cultivate. I'm deeply grateful for your humility and grace toward me and your service to the team over the last fifteen years. It's a priceless gift you've given.

Krista Kotrla, I'll never forget sitting on the back porch with the leadership team as you asked to take the helm of the 2011 retreat. From laying the groundwork for our mission to opening our eyes to the way Block Imaging offers a second chance at life in healthcare, you brought conviction and language that were powerful in catalyzing the rebirth of a company. So proud of the leader you're becoming and the impact you're making in organizations around the world. You continue to be a sister who's living a life worthy of an adverb.

ACKNOWLEDGMENTS

Anita Philip, as a friend and the director of human resources for those first eight years, you brought extraordinary steadiness and wisdom to a young and growing leader in desperate need of both. I'm forever grateful for your belief and investment in my life and our organization. I cried the day you shared it was time to move on, and I've missed working alongside you every day since.

Zack, you recommended the shoes that I wore on the run that greenlit this book—to which your response was "Finally." Your belief and encouragement in my life are prolific, from the coin at Great 8 to the way you love my family and choose "with" every single time. I can't wait to shoot our age together on the golf course someday. And please be sure to tell JB I'm sorry about his jet ski.

Siemens Healthineers and CommonSpirit Health Teams, your recognition, appreciation, and ultimately protection of Block Imaging's culture and story have been nothing short of remarkable. Thank you for the way you've supported our family, our leaders, and the team at large. Excited to see our teams continue to work together to build and serve in unprecedented ways.

Josh and Linds, your invitation to relocate, launch a business, rehab homes, and work alongside the people of urban Muncie changed everything. My view of life, leadership, and meaningful work was forever altered by that season and the choices you led us into.

Andrew and Leslie, you taught me to take risks and step into the water before it started to move. Watching you lead with courage and conviction bestowed something in me that wasn't there before.

Jerome and Crystal, you've loved and accepted us incredibly over the last ten years. Your grace, kindness, and invitation into family when we were trying to find home in Lansing was such a gift.

Steve and Paula, your wisdom, belief, and encouragement have been more valuable than you know. You paved the way for us to "follow the joy" and exchange "should do" for "get to do" over and over again.

Dr. Marvin Williams, thank you for inviting us to fish with wet nets in 2011: It's been a blast fishing together.

Wes Cate, your presence and perspective have shaped me more than you know. You helped me see leadership not as something to master but as something to steward—with humility, clarity, and courage. Your ability to draw truth to the surface and lead me with wisdom toward joy has sharpened my thinking and softened my edges.

Brandi, Trevor, Zack, Mackenzie, James, Joal, Andy, Ben, Kevin, Tyler, Chris, Amy, Nicole, Eric, Becky, David, thank you for your willingness to help bring *People Matter at Work* to life by sharing your stories. You were the reason for creating the culture described in these pages long before the idea of a book came to be.

To all the **vendors** and **customers** of Block Imaging over the years, I'm so grateful for your trust in and support

ACKNOWLEDGMENTS

of a once little family business in Lansing, Michigan. The opportunity to serve you over nearly thirty years has been a gift.

And to those who journeyed with me over the six years of bringing this book to life, Joy Eggerichs Reed, Beth Graybill, Amelia Graves, Andy Bailey, Dan Trego, Becky Nesbitt, Kia Harris, the entire Forefront Team, Scott Harris, Davon Salvagno, and the Grey + Miller Team. Each of you is remarkably talented, and I'm thankful for your support and tenacity in honing and ultimately sharing *People Matter at Work* with the world.

To the countless others who've played impactful roles in shaping my life and the Block Imaging story, thank you. The view from your shoulders is magnificent.

INTRODUCTION

The Problem: A Case of the Mondays

I know it might sound crazy, but I was raised in a home where work was a good thing. I never once heard my dad complain about his hour commute, and when we were young, my brothers and I would fight over who got to mow the lawn. And yet, as I moved through high school, graduated college, and entered the workforce, it quickly became clear that my experience and view of work weren't the norm. As a young adult, I quickly began to realize that for most, W-O-R-K has become the four-letter expletive of our time.

Today, most people work because they *have to*, give only what they're *supposed to*, and leave as soon as they're *allowed to*. How's that for inspiration? On a good day, it feels like a transactional exchange of time and effort for a paycheck and fringe benefits, and it's my suspicion that if you're like most people, you're better able to describe what the tough days look like than I am. What does it say about work that we live in a place and time when phrases like "a case of the Mondays" and "working for the weekend" are commonplace in their negative portrayal of work? If the walls of countless organizations could talk, they'd say that trust has been broken, office politics reign supreme, teamwork is a lost art, and the thought of actually *enjoying* work—let alone *thriving* in it—feels like a fantasy.

Has Work Always Been This Way?

Always and *never* are dangerous words, but we'd be crazy not to acknowledge the enormous shifts in work and commerce over the last hundred years. The Industrial Revolution introduced assembly lines and new modes of transportation. While we might have imagined that the car would simply take us to the same places faster, the reality is that the automobile increased not only speed but also distance. Planes, trains, and automobiles joined together with the growth of public corporations to stretch the distance between shareholders and employees like never before. The scope and scale of these public enterprises ushered in a new world of layered management structures and provided "big" organizations an outsized role in shaping economics, work, and life.

INTRODUCTION

Along with scale, distance, and mid-level management, the pursuit of creating shareholder wealth ushered in a chase for quarterly earnings, far too often at the expense of people's well-being and the company's long-term health. While it might seem obvious, **organizations that disproportionately prioritize shareholder wealth in ninety-day increments will have a tough time creating a culture where people thrive and in turn bring their best.**

And yet, all over the world, day after day, the corporate wheel spins as employees scramble for promotions, pay, and a sense of purpose while bosses look to squeeze the most out of their people on their way to the top.

Is It Really This Bad?

I wouldn't have spent the last fifteen years practicing and six years writing if I didn't think we had a big problem on our hands. While I don't know your specific situation or company, anecdotal conversations and broad swaths of data indicate that the problem is both real and growing.

Let's look at what Gallup, the most broad and respected surveyor in the team engagement space, has to say about people's view of work. Depending on your experience, you might think that when modern workplace engagement survey results peaked, 60 percent of people were engaged at work. Or maybe you're slightly more suspicious (or cynical), and you're more likely to guess that 50ish percent of people were engaged at work. Well, take a deep breath because even those of us who buffered our answers weren't even close. In Gallup's pre-pandemic 2020 survey, a mere one-third of US employees were deemed "engaged." And that was a *record* year!

If you assume that this is just a US phenomenon, it's time to recalibrate. The global statistics are, for the most part, worse. In New Zealand and Southeast Asia, engagement hovers in the low to mid twenties; in Europe, between 2020 and 2023, the results were in the low teens. Whether it's one in three or one in eight, it's safe to say that with the majority in the realm of indifferent or actively disengaged, there's some serious gold in these hills.

An Invitation from a Fellow Practitioner

When my leadership journey began amid doubt and uncertainty over the course of a weekend, my primary focus was on keeping the company afloat. I sure as heck wasn't thinking about writing a book about it someday! But one day of practice turned into a month, then into a year. Now, a decade and a half later, I'm excited to share what we've learned.

As we leave the starting gate together, it's important to highlight that this book is written *from one practitioner to another*. While writing and speaking have been both energizing and refining, most of my workweek is still dedicated to leading several teams as we serve the

INTRODUCTION

healthcare community around the world. Our roles and contexts undoubtedly differ, but you and I share the reality that true leadership is rooted in *practice*. Just as doctors practice medicine to help people live healthier lives, leaders rise every day to make their teams and organizations stronger, healthier, and more successful. Our practice stems from our convictions; the stories and principles that follow didn't come from MBA coursework or academic theory but from the unshakable belief that there has to be a better way for people to spend upward of *eighty thousand hours* of their adult lives.

The second important thing to mention is that many of the ideas, structures, and principles found in this book weren't formed at the beginning of the journey but were discovered *organically* and *cultivated* over time. For every story shared here, there are hundreds more to choose from and countless more I've never heard. Even after more than fifteen years of living out the three T's in pursuit of creating an organization with *people matter* at its core, it's only in the last several years that the visual and prescriptive nature of the We-Cycle has come to life. If this book serves in any way to shape your mindset around how you see people and approach leadership, it will have been well worth the effort.

People Matter at Work is a blend of stories and principles. I'm all too aware of our ever-waning collective attention span, so the book is designed to be read either start to finish or in standalone chunks. For those who struggle to read a book cover to cover, I encourage you to use the table of contents to skip around if you're looking to home in on one specific piece of the We-Cycle. However you decide to join us, I'm so pleased to be a part of your leadership journey.

Three Pitfalls

As we continue on, it's important to highlight a couple of traps to avoid as you read.

Pitfall #1: Comparison

Drafting is a technique used by cyclists, swimmers, speed skaters, and even semi-truck drivers. You may have seen athletes tuck in behind someone else to take advantage of the windbreak they provide, which reduces resistance and effort. Comparison, on the other hand, has a similar effect to a headwind. In a world obsessed with comparison, I invite you to "draft" instead.

The comparison trap might sound like this:

- "But Josh, you're in the healthcare space."
- "But Josh, you're the president of the organization."
- "But Josh, your organization is much smaller (or bigger) than ours."

INTRODUCTION

In many cases, comparison carries a far higher propensity to justify inaction than to stir action. So, instead of comparing, why not draft? You'll benefit from others' experiences without the full resistance of doing it alone. So much of my own growth has come from drafting behind others' wisdom and ideas. As I mentioned earlier, my reading list is filled with thought leaders I've never met, but they've broken more wind for me than they'll ever know. (And yes, I see the humor in that phrase!) A quick piece of life advice as a parent of teenagers: It's always better when someone breaks wind *for* you rather than *on* you.

Pitfall #2: Context

It's easy to hear someone's story and think, "That won't work here" or "That's not authentic to who I am." If an idea you read here doesn't fit your context or feels too fluffy, modify it and make it your own. Rather than dismissing something due to a contextual difference, I'd encourage you to focus on the overarching principles, then adjust and adapt them to suit your unique situation. If you want to bring families together outside of work hours but a drive-in movie night, Friendsgiving, kickball game, company-wide retreat, or roller-skating party doesn't make sense (yup, those are real things here at Block Imaging), get creative! Whether you're in financial services or running a nonprofit, the key is to tailor rather than dismiss. It doesn't matter if your team is mostly white collar, blue collar, or no collar; creating a place where *people matter* invites us into care and creativity. It can be done, and it's worth it!

Pitfall #3: Completion

Shaping culture is never "done." Like remodeling, it's often messier than expected and takes twice as long as you might think. When we first began our journey toward creating a healthy culture in 2011, I thought it would take eighteen to twenty-four months to get the organization headed in the right direction. While we saw progress in those first few weeks and months, it took longer than expected to really feel the wind in our sails. Deep and enduring cultural change requires a mix of intentionality and endurance. *That's why you're here!*

From one leader to another: Don't be discouraged if resistance is high and progress is slow. Stay the course. In time, you'll see transformation begin to take place, and you'll feel the impact in people's lives, in their level of engagement, and ultimately in the organization's performance.

So without further introduction or fanfare, but with great excitement, anticipation, and belief in the leader you're becoming, let's cannonball into the pool and swim toward creating a workplace culture where *people matter*.

PART I

Tripping into Leadership

Before we discuss how we as leaders create a culture where *people matter* more, I thought it would be helpful to provide some background on how we got here. (Spoiler alert: Sometimes it's as surprising for the leader as it is for the team.)

CHAPTER 1

Sales Rep to President

I was born and raised in Michigan, the fourth of five kids with two more bonus brothers to come. My mom had her tubes tied before I was born, so suffice it to say, I've always been up for overcoming obstacles. Even at forty-four, it never gets old watching my parents cringe when I refer to myself as their "favorite accident."

Even as a child, I remember loving work and being drawn to people. As a twelve-year-old, when most of my friends were drawn to *Mario Bros.*, I was dreaming up and executing a plan to pick strawberries and sell them door to door. Entrepreneurship felt like a video game or a sport of my own design. From ages thirteen to fifteen I had the opportunity to work with friends at a nearby cider mill. There was so much to learn through pricing pumpkins, filling cider jugs, making donuts, giving pony rides, and even wearing a Barney costume (from which no amount of fresh-baked donuts could overpower the stench of on a hot day).

In high school, I juggled several jobs that had a lot to teach about marketing and customer service. Flipping burgers and running the drive-thru at a local burger joint, managing an indoor golf simulator league, and waiting tables at Cracker Barrel were just a few of the experiences that would begin shaping my view of work and business. Every night, I'd come home with a stack of pancakes and a handful of $1's and $5's that I'd use to repay my dad for my first car, a sweet, emerald-green two-door Ford Tempo.

Fast-forward to college. I packed up that trusty Tempo and headed off to Taylor University, a small liberal arts school in Indiana. I was hoping to make new friends and earn a degree in business, but little did I know, I would meet my wife, Lacey, during Welcome Weekend—before classes even started. I'll never forget seeing her in her sparkly jeans and orange bandana at the freshman square dance. We were too far away from the caller to hear his instructions, so I took her by the hand, and we made our way to the front of the gym. Twenty-five years later, and the rest is history. What can I say? I've always been drawn to striking while the iron's hot!

People Matter 1.0

As Lacey and I started our sophomore year, we began spending time with a group of friends who were passionate about urban community development. While most students focused on enjoying their college years, Lacey and I were already planning for life after graduation. One of the biggest challenges facing the urban core of Muncie, Indiana, was a lack of meaningful work. Building on my work experiences and a few relatives in the service space, my brother-in-law (also named Josh) and I saw an opportunity for job creation and economic stimulation through starting a window-washing and house-cleaning company.

Toward the latter part of my sophomore year, Josh and I decided to launch NRG Service Industries with the purpose of employing people who had otherwise struggled to find work for various reasons—whether it be a lack of education, opportunity, or perhaps past mistakes. Josh ran the daily operations while I maintained a full course load, handled the bookkeeping, and brainstormed about how to grow the business.

Lacey and I got married between our junior and senior years and moved into a one-bedroom apartment in downtown Muncie. Our monthly rent was $400. Ever an opportunistic couple, the landlord hired us to vacuum the staircases and three floors of hallways every Sunday for $25 a week. We were kids new to paying rent, and I'll never forget when we forgot to send in our rent check and received a $50 late fee. Lacey had tears in her eyes realizing we'd have to throw two weeks of vacuuming down the drain to cover the late fee!

Less than a year later, we bought our first home at 1625 Jefferson Street for $18,500. It was a 1,000-square-foot, shotgun-style house that we'd spend hundreds and hundreds of hours remodeling. For some new marriages, remodeling a house from the 1960s would be a nightmare, but for Lacey and me, we were having an absolute blast learning to work as a team and lean on each other's strengths.

I will never forget the smell of the wood stripper we used to restore every inch of historic woodwork or the sound of the sandpaper as we resurfaced the pine floors of our first real home together. This was a formative season in our lives, filled with lots of long days and really hard but fulfilling work.

The Early Years

Right after graduation, I jumped into the day-to-day operations of the window-washing business. One early moment that stands out in my memory is picking up a father of five for his first day of work. We began the day by stopping to grab a belt at the store so that he'd be able to holster his window-washing equipment. While money might be the most obvious reason people get a job, it didn't take long to see that work offered so much more than just a paycheck; it also created a sense of pride and purpose for those given the opportunity to develop skills and be part of a team. Over time, we noticed how a steady job brought stability to families that, without consistent employment, were prone to move from house to house and school to school. This experience left an indelible mark on my passion for how business and work could profoundly transform the lives of people and their families.

As we prepared to start our own family, Lacey and I decided to purchase and remodel a home across the street three doors down. With a bit of back-and-forth, the seller budged from his $10,000 asking price to accept our $5,500 cash offer. The back door had been kicked in, and animals were living in the house, but that didn't deter us. Over the next several months, I worked on the house early in the morning and washed windows throughout the day. Lacey and I would keep jamming on the house after the workday and late into most evenings. Fourteen-hour days on the weekend were standard in the winter and spring of 2006 as we expanded the second story and remodeled every inch of that home in preparation for our baby girl.

Looking back, we were living our best life. We were on mission. We loved our neighborhood, were surrounded by lifelong friends, and had poured blood, sweat, and tears into what we thought would be our forever home. This season was essential to who we were becoming with a deep love for people and a passion for hard work at the forefront.

We also learned a lot from our share of mistakes. As we started demolition on the inside of the house, I thought it would be wise to save on the cost of dumpsters. Instead of throwing everything out, we created what began as a *small* burn pile in the backyard to rid us of the lath strips that held up the plaster of the mid-1900s home. Burn pile in an urban neighborhood? Yup, that's right. Impatient as always, I decided the fire could handle *just a little bit more*.

Anyway, before I knew it, sirens were coming from all directions. I grabbed the hose and tried to reduce the evidence as the fire trucks pulled up and saw what was going on.

I wish I could tell you that this was the only time my friends at the fire department "dropped by." The picture of the firefighter is the same person who would eventually become the mayor of Muncie, so I like to think of it as nothing more than a campaign stop. As kind as they were, let me assure you of one thing: When they put out a fire, *they put out a fire*! Each time, I'd thank them but think to myself, "Did you really have to use that much water?" Didn't they understand how hard it was to rebuild my discount disintegration chamber after they'd flooded the backyard?

Less than a year after completing the remodel, we welcomed our daughter, Anneliese, into the world. As things were evolving in both our family and the business, I felt a stirring inside that led to my partner, Josh, continuing forward in the business while I transitioned into a sales role with the medical imaging business that my dad started when I was a freshman in high school.

Joining Block Imaging in a regional sales role seemed like a perfect fit, creating a path for me to provide for our family while we continued to invest in our community in Indiana. Little did I know that in a few short years, this career change would set in motion a far bigger transition than Lacey and I had imagined or planned for.

Starting Blocks

Prior to venturing out and starting the company, my dad spent twenty-five years following in his father's footsteps in the coffee roasting and distribution business. With a business plan in hand and hopes of launching a coffeehouse well before Starbucks exploded and third-wave shops came onto the scene, Dad met with a potential investor with the hope of launching Jocundry's Coffee.

It just so happened that the investor owned an imaging equipment trade business, and while they were out looking for locations for the shop, he asked Dad about his interest in an interim sales role for his struggling radiology equipment brokering business. In an effort to put food on the table, Dad took him up on the offer as an "in-between" of sorts. Just as Dad was getting familiar enough with the imaging business to put some deals together, the owner decided to file for bankruptcy.

While the dream of opening Jocundry's Coffee remained in the back of his mind, Dad found some success in brokering medical equipment to Asia and South America and decided to purchase the database and start Block Imaging in 1997. With humble beginnings in the three-seasons room of our home in Dewitt, Michigan, Block Imaging's "headquarters" soon expanded to a five-hundred-square-foot office across the street from the local (by the hour) hot-tub rental joint. Over the first decade, Block Imaging grew significantly. What started as a way to feed our family would soon become one of the most trusted and recognized names in the world for pre-owned medical imaging equipment, parts, and service.

Changes on the Horizon

Jason Crawford and I had attended the same high school prior to him joining the United States Merchant Marine Academy after graduation. Following a short stint at a logistics company, Jason joined Block Imaging in 2002 as a project manager and was Block's fifth team member. Over the next decade, Jason would become a key leader in the organization. In 2009, seeing Jason's passion for the parts and service business, Dad offered him the opportunity to launch Block Imaging Parts and Service as a daughter company of Block Imaging International.

Even though I knew Jason from high school, since joining the company from Muncie, we hadn't worked together much. From 2006 to 2010, I sold imaging equipment remotely by day while we continued to pour ourselves into the Muncie community through housing rehabilitation, addiction recovery, tutoring, and even purchasing and demolishing a strip club that had become a haven for drugs and violence. So much of what we had dreamt about in the early years was coming to fruition.

But back in Lansing, after more than a decade of rapid growth, and while the launch of Jason's parts and service business was off to a great start, Block Imaging's core equipment business was beginning to lose momentum. Moving at two different speeds and at very different stages of the organizational life cycle, the mothership and the start-up began subtly drifting in different directions.

During a passing conversation with my dad in the spring of 2010, it became clear that the leadership team (which I wasn't yet part of) was struggling with a lack of clarity and unified direction. I can't recall exactly what sparked the moment—and it still feels a bit surreal to think about it all these years later—but on a whim, I asked my dad if he'd be open to me facilitating the leadership team meetings for a season.

Looking back, asking to facilitate meetings from Indiana before Zoom or Teams existed was as absurd as grabbing Lacey's hand at the freshman square dance. But my dad didn't flinch. He said he would run the idea by the leaders, and a week or two later Dad shared that the team was warm enough to the idea that he'd like to give it a shot. Neither of us had any idea that facilitating this team over the next fifteen months would provide a profound opportunity to learn the business, build bridges, and prepare for the unimaginable climb that lay ahead.

You might be noticing a theme of "little did I know" in this season. These moments were all just precursors to a much more unexpected transition on the horizon.

Black Thursday

It became clear as I began facilitating the team over the next couple of months that the gap between our financial targets and actual performance was growing at an untenable pace. Having expanded from a fledgling enterprise run by Dad in a home office with no revenue to a team of fifty with $30 million in revenue over thirteen years, this was entirely new ground for the leaders. While I was new to the facilitator role, it didn't take a Harvard MBA to recognize that we had only two options to bridge the gap: increase revenue or reduce expenses. When it became clear that boosting margins through more sales wasn't a reasonable short-term solution, the team turned their attention to cost reductions.

Over the following weeks, each leader came forward with their proposed cuts. Initially, the savings came from trade shows and technology expenditures, but soon the conversation shifted from vendors to people. While it appeared that we'd initially met our expense-cutting goals without laying anyone off, I could sense a lingering tension and apprehension. In response to what felt like an elephant in the room, I posed a question.

"Do you think we should go further?"

Little did I know (there it is again) that such a simple question would open a door into one of the darkest and most painful moments in Block Imaging's history. The leadership team responded with a confident and collective nod that they thought we needed to make deeper cuts. Within hours, a plan was put in place to lay off 12 percent of the team. The following day, department leaders moved through headquarters, one after another, rocking people's careers and lives.

All these years later, it's no less haunting than it was on what would become known around Block Imaging as "Black Thursday."

Hindsight: Is It Always 20/20?

In hindsight, I wish I could click undo on that leadership moment. While "Do you think we should go further?" might seem like a reasonable question for a facilitator to pose, it was deeply incongruent with who we'd been as a company. While *people matter* had yet to rise to the surface as our company mission, since the beginning Dad had always wanted to lead Block Imaging in a way that cared for people.

For years after the meeting that led to Black Thursday, I took solace in the fact that technically I didn't make the decision. After all, I was just the facilitator. But in recent years, I've come to recognize and more fully own my critical role in shaping that fateful day. While it can be easy to point fingers or find someone or something to hide behind, looking back I lacked the maturity, foresight, and vision to imagine a better way forward. In turn, I missed the opportunity to ask a far better question in that transformative moment: "What action should we take to balance both caring for our people and supporting the business into the future?"

While we live in a culture of Monday morning quarterbacking in which criticism aimed toward leaders (some rightfully earned) is at an all-time high, every mistake holds a paradox within. On one hand, seeing the impact on everyone involved was gut-wrenchingly painful. And, while there's no "easy" or "rewind" button for decisions like this one, even in our darkest hour, failure can be an influential teacher. Watching this decision play out and seeing what happens in a culture when trust is broken and security is lost provided a priceless leadership lesson. It came at a great cost and yet would be a powerful influence in shaping the leader I was becoming.

I'd seen the power of creating meaningful work in those early days in Muncie, and sadly, this decision brought about quite the opposite effect. And it didn't just impact those who were departing. There was no question that this move ripped the rug right out from underneath their feet, but it didn't stop there. Those who remained were left with questions like "When might it happen again?" and "Will I be next?" As difficult as this season was, the magnitude and timing of the layoff would be more illuminating for me as a young leader than I knew at the time.

Plot Twist

In January of 2011, after facilitating the leadership team for just over twelve months, Lacey and I found ourselves reflecting on the previous year and dreaming about the next one on our drive home after a New Year's celebration with my side of the family in Michigan. Our conversation drifted to our desire to move south someday to escape the blustery Indiana winters. Then, out of nowhere, Lacey said, "What if we moved to Michigan, babe?" As Clark Griswold says when his cousin Eddie shows up unannounced in the movie *Christmas Vacation*, "If I woke up tomorrow with my head sewn to the carpet, I wouldn't be more surprised than I am now."

We had been rooted in Muncie since college, and things were going well with my remote sales role at Block. We loved our newly renovated home and were elbow deep in parenting an almost four-year-old (Anneliese) and an eighteen-month-old (Jamin). We had poured our lives into the people of Muncie and had worked to establish deep roots that we thought would keep us planted there at least until our kids graduated high school. *Michigan? Really?* Lacey's comment didn't make any sense to me, and it was especially shocking to hear it coming from my wife, who had never wanted to move any farther north or away from her family. And yet, for some reason, our wheels started turning.

In the coming months, Lacey and I began to recognize that we had already slowly begun releasing our leadership roles to others in the Muncie community. Now I was starting to wonder if that subconscious "letting go" of leadership was in anticipation of something new on the horizon. Despite our aspirations for warmer weather, Lacey and I began seriously considering a move north.

Out of the Blue

In February of 2011, Jason Crawford and I were driving together to Cincinnati to meet with a customer about the challenges they were facing with their MRI. Somewhere around Findlay, Ohio, out of the blue, Jason asked, "Have you and Lacey ever thought about relocating to Lansing?"

The timing of Jason's question caught me off guard in a big way and put me on the spot. I had to decide quickly whether to share openly what Lacey and I had been thinking about. Ever the straight shooter, I shared that we'd just started talking about the idea. Jason's response would illuminate the extraordinary abundance mindset he carries to the core of his being. If even a hint of power and control were on his mind, or if he feared that my relocation to headquarters might threaten his position, he could've easily steered us away by emphasizing how great Muncie was for us or perhaps by sharing the disadvantages of Michigan taxes and roads or the challenges of being closer to family. While there's an element of truth to each point, that's not who Jason is. The dude didn't even think twice.

"I think it'd be great!" he responded.

As we drove back from Cincinnati after meeting with the customer, we chatted a bit further about the impact and implications of a possible move for our family. At the time, we had no sense that this conversation would be pivotal in setting the foundation for one of the most fulfilling, impactful friendships and business partnerships I could've ever imagined and would ultimately pave the way for the book you're now listening to or holding in your hand.

After returning home to Muncie, the conversation about relocating progressed. Lacey and I couldn't shake the notion that the journey to Michigan was one we were supposed to take. We couldn't articulate precisely why, but with tears rolling down our faces, we ventured north over Memorial Day Weekend 2011, just five months after our initial conversation. The plan was to continue in my role as a sales rep at the company and begin facilitating the leadership team in person.

Have We Made a Huge Mistake?

In the early weeks and months after the move, we missed our community in Indiana deeply. It didn't take long for us to wonder if we'd made a colossal mistake. Amid the loneliness and confusion, I drove to the office on an ordinary Friday morning in September, ready to finish the week strong. But instead, over the course of the day, it became clear that Dad would be transitioning from his role as president. I left the office that day with my mind spinning, unsure of what was next.

It just so happened that Lacey and I had been invited to dinner at a coworker's house the next night. As fate would have it, Jason and his family were also there. Just like on our drive to Cincinnati, Jason's "spidey senses" could clearly tell something was up. He asked a few questions about the weekend, and what began as small talk turned into full-on curiosity. Not one for conversational dodgeball, I decided to step outside and give Dad a call. I shared that Jason was asking questions and that it was getting uncomfortable having to sidestep and keep something so impactful from him. Dad agreed to give Jason a call, and a few minutes later, Jason and I connected privately in the backyard. Unsure of how the conversation with my dad had unfolded, I asked Jason what my dad had said. Without knowing that he was the first to share the news, Jason said, "Your dad told me he'd be naming you president of the organization on Monday."

Thump-thump.

Thump-thump.

Thump-thump.

My heartbeat echoed in my ears as I tried to maintain my composure. While I was aware that Dad would be stepping back from the company, I didn't know he would ask me to lead it moving forward. Jason and I chatted briefly in the backyard before rejoining everyone for dinner. As you might imagine, my brain was going a million miles a minute.

After saying our goodbyes and getting the kids to sleep, I lay in bed staring at the ceiling as I imagined what the days and weeks ahead would hold. It wasn't that I hadn't considered being part of the next generation of leadership at Block Imaging *someday*. It's just that I never envisioned it would be at twenty-nine years old having worked at headquarters for only four months. When I had thought about preparing for a transition someday, I imagined the timeline to be more like seventy-two *months*, not seventy-two *hours*.

While we knew our lives were about to get twist-turned upside down (any *Fresh Prince* fans out there?), a weight lifted off my chest when Lacey looked at me and said, "This must be why we're here." That realization didn't instantly make Lansing home, but it brought a sense of peace amid the loneliness of having left so much behind. For the first time, I was beginning to understand why we'd felt such a strong pull to move our family to Michigan.

On Sunday, my dad gathered my siblings and their spouses to share his plan. While there was much to process and prepare for, Monday morning came quickly. Walking into Block Imaging's headquarters, I saw Emily

Jones, a sales support specialist I'd hired just after arriving in Michigan, standing outside the conference room. We stepped inside, and I privately shared with her what was about to take place: Dad would be transitioning to the chairman role, and I'd be stepping into the role of president. I let her know that we'd be moving offices, and I asked if she could set up the conference room for a company-wide announcement at 9 a.m.

While Emily still doesn't think it was that big of a deal and to this day wishes this story didn't make the book, I'll never forget that she didn't hesitate or stop to ask about her role, title, or pay. She understood the significance of the moment, and while some would've stressed out or even thought about leveraging it, with presence and poise, Emily looked at me and simply said, "Got it." That sincere response revealed more about her character than any interview ever could. While it was a massive transition for me, that morning would serve as a decisive first step in her own journey toward becoming a remarkable executive assistant for the decade to come and now, nearly fifteen years later, our director of parts sales.

As I reflect back on that morning, I remember feeling like I was being called up from a high school baseball team to the major leagues overnight. With a flurry of emotions swirling in and around me as the entire company began to gather following the last-minute meeting invite, the first pitch was on the way, and it was time to swing. After my dad spoke, I shared a few remarks, and class was in session for my first semester toward a fast-tracked street MBA.

With the aftershock of Black Thursday still in the air, I could sense the team's uneasiness in the midst of this sudden leadership transition. As I walked through the office that morning, uncertainty loomed as it felt like the whole organization had been shaken like a snow globe. While I had worked alongside the sales reps and leadership team from afar over the past several years, from a leadership perspective I was at best an unknown commodity and at worst a twenty-nine-year-old who got the job only because of my last name.

While the road ahead looked daunting, there was little time for planning or space for hesitation; it was game time.

Keeping It Real

David
Technical Operations Manager | 4 years at Block

I joined Block in November, just weeks after the annual retreat. At the time, *people matter* felt like a nice sentiment—similar to the mission statements I'd seen at many hospitals I'd worked in. Throughout that first year, I had witnessed acts of care and generosity from leadership, but the phrase hadn't truly come alive for me yet.

That changed the following October, when I experienced the retreat for myself. It was a powerful, eye-opening moment. Looking back, I realized those earlier acts of kindness weren't just surface-level. They were authentic expressions of *people matter*. A few days after returning, I walked into my leader's office and said, "I'm in. I don't know what it means yet, but I want to do more."

Before coming to Block, I'd gone through two stressful and careless company mergers. Both left a bad taste. Josh knew that about my past. So, before Block's joint venture announcement, he pulled me aside and told me personally—giving me space to process and respond. He didn't have to do that, but he did. Because he was thoughtful. Because he wanted to be transparent. Because we were in it *together*.

I'll also never forget a Friday when I was onsite at a hospital, knee-deep in a complex equipment issue. Days had turned into late nights, and nothing was working. That afternoon, after another failed attempt, I hit a wall and fired off a series of frustrated texts to my leader. Instead of reacting, he listened, asked thoughtful questions, and helped me find a way forward. When I got home later that day, there was a handwritten card and a small gift waiting for me. That one gesture reminded me: I was seen, I was appreciated, and I wasn't alone.

Block has changed the way I work and the way I *see* work. I came from a world where profit was king, placed above people, patients, and everything else. Block could not be more different. Here, people are cared for with deep intentionality. You're encouraged to stretch, supported if you fall, and reminded that your well-being matters—both on and off the clock. I still find myself recalibrating. But I come home a better person than I used to.

We're pushed to grow, to take risks, to do meaningful work, and we do it in a culture that gives permission to fail. We fall short sometimes, but what's different here is this: Win or lose, we go through it *together*.

This year, the word that sums up *People Matter at Work* for me is *intentionality*. Being thoughtful about how we work *with* each other. Stopping to ask how someone's really doing. Looking for moments to help people feel seen. That's where trust is built. That's where culture takes root. And that's what makes Block different.

Nicole
Procurement Manager | 8 years at Block

Shortly after I started at Block, our team launched a book club. At first, I didn't take it seriously—I assumed no one really cared what I thought. But then my leader called on me directly to share my opinion. What followed surprised me; there was encouragement, engagement, and genuine interest in what I had to say. Meeting after meeting, I was invited to speak up, and slowly, my confidence grew. Looking back, that early experience shaped everything. Without it, I'm not sure I'd be where I am today. Now, one of my favorite parts of the job is helping others find that same confidence and reminding them that they have a voice and a seat at the table.

Block is unlike any other company I've worked for. Our CEO, president, and senior leaders don't hide behind titles. They share financials, ask for your input, and even check in on your spouse and kids. Over the past year and a half, our team has gone through a lot of change. And yet, in the midst of the transition, I've received handwritten notes from leaders recognizing what I've carried and thanking me for navigating the team through it all. Those small moments make a big impact. They remind me that what I do is seen.

I've remained at Block for eight years because of the culture and because of the people. I've built real friendships here. My coworkers have walked with me through every season of life: getting engaged and married, getting a dog, having a baby, and even losing someone I loved. They've shown up for all of it. I can't imagine finding that kind of care and consistency anywhere else.

I'm not the same person I was eight years ago, and I'm thankful for that. I've grown in my career but also in my confidence, resilience, and sense of purpose. I feel seen, safe, and significant here. We get to work hard, make a difference, and have fun along the way. And in the end, we're part of something that matters—helping people get the scans they need and supporting the team that makes it all happen.

To me, *People Matter at Work* is about *opportunity*, the opportunity to grow, to connect, to become who you're meant to be, and to make a meaningful impact along the way.

CHAPTER 2

The Me-Cycle and the Gift of Humble Pie

The Culprit: The Me-Cycle

Before we take the story further, let's explore a cycle that expresses how lots of bosses and employees operate, which provides insight into why most people are disengaged at work. Every relationship moves in a cycle of sorts: One person acts in a certain way, the other responds, and the cycle continues. We've all seen healthy relationships in which people love and care for one another, and we've all likely seen toxic relationships in which one or both people involved treat each other terribly.

At the core, one of the major differences between energizing and depleting relationships is the person we're focused on and the lens we're looking through. The best analogy that comes to mind is the difference between looking *into* a mirror versus looking *through* a window. When we stare into a mirror at close range, we're most likely to see and focus on ourselves: the hair that's out of place or the wrinkle that's beginning to deepen. But when we look through a window, even if we catch a glimpse of our own reflection, our natural and primary focus is what's on the other side of the pane of glass.

While this applies to any friendship, and most especially to marriages, let's think about it in terms of workplace enjoyment and engagement. While we'll spend the better part of this book aimed toward the solution, the problem warrants some explanation. Allow me to introduce the Me-Cycle.

As you can see in the graphic, in a culture driven by the Me-Cycle, everyone is focused on themselves and looking to see what they can *get* out of the deal. When a "Me-First" mentality runs wild, our attitudes and actions communicate that our needs are at the center, and we begin treating people as if they exist to give us what we want. This is the opposite of what Emily Jones did when I shared that I was about to become president of the company. She saw what those around her needed, and she leapt into action. Emily broke the Me-Cycle before it even got moving.

One thing that's important for us to remember is that those in authority are the initiators of any workplace cycle, for better or for worse. By looking into a mirror and focusing primarily on their own wants and needs, the "leader" (read *boss*) sets the Me-Cycle in motion. The needs of the "team" (read *employees*) are secondary to ensuring the boss's power, position, pay, and prestige grow.

Unsurprisingly, when the Me-Cycle is churning away, employees feel unsafe, unseen, and unsuccessful, and they respond by focusing exclusively on themselves. Left unchecked and with no way out, the Me-Cycle spirals. The boss is viewed as selfish and controlling, and as the employees focus on self-preservation, they get labeled as lazy, selfish, and entitled. Bosses turn to command and control in an attempt to get what they want. In the end, both parties become disenchanted, and everyone loses, including the organization.

While the Me-Cycle is painful for all involved, the good news is that *it doesn't have to be this way*. Here's a quick recap:

1. Many organizations are stuck in the Me-Cycle.
2. The Me-Cycle starts with the person in authority.
3. There's a better way.

Humble Pie

Back to the story. In the days and weeks that followed the announcement, uncertainty hung in the air like a thick fog. On the outside, everyone seemed calm, collected, and ready for the transition. But beneath that surface, I could sense the undercurrent of concern and instability. It was as though the team had stepped off of a rocky boat ride and were unsure of how to regain steady footing on land. And who could blame them? After all, the trust foundational to Block Imaging's success had been rattled twice in six short months, first on Black Thursday and now with my sudden transition. I knew that if we were to move forward together, it was crucial to regain *trust* and *confidence* in our leaders.

My dad had been the founder and president of Block Imaging for its first fifteen years. When he passed the torch to me, he was sixty-one years old with a master's degree in accounting, decades of business experience, and a deep understanding of the medical imaging industry. In contrast, I was an eager twenty-nine-year-old who had been with the company for just a few years. I could sense the questions and doubts swirling in people's minds:

Is this really happening?
What's going to change, and what's going to stay the same?
How will decisions be made going forward?
Does Josh even know what he's doing?

I couldn't blame them for their questions and concerns. So much change had unfolded so quickly. After all, I was asking some of the very same questions myself. It was easy to feel overwhelmed as I spent time with team leaders and learned just how much there was that I *didn't* know as I moved from focusing exclusively on sales to being responsible for the entire organization: sales, accounting, IT, marketing, human resources, and an office in Japan. From benefits to hiring to the international side of the business and all that comes with it, there were so many areas I had yet to dip my toes into. At the time, public speaking was pretty nerve-racking, and the weight of responsibility for the business was as real as can be. I could spell *MRI* and had sold quite a few over the years, but I had no idea how to turn one on, let alone conduct a patient scan, and I still don't to this day. To say I had a lot to learn about our business would be the understatement of the century. While the team—notably Jason Crawford, my brothers, and our other leaders—was incredibly gracious and helpful, I was keenly aware of my inexperience.

Many leaders on my team were longtime colleagues and friends of my dad. Some had been in the industry for decades. In the midst of weighing my strengths and battling my insecurities, a vexing question cycled through my mind as I sought to gain some leadership footing: "Would anyone take a twenty-nine-year-old newbie seriously, let alone follow me?" On the difficult days, when a challenge rose to the surface that I'd never seen before and people were looking to me for direction, the internal monologue of "you got this job only because you're the founder's son" ran through my head on a loop.

And yet, despite all my insecurities and limitations, I was reminded of some of the strengths and experiences that would prove beneficial in the season ahead: I had a passion for business, a love for meaningful work, and a heart for people. Much of this was bestowed by my parents and put into practice through working a number of jobs in high school, starting a business in college, and taking all sorts of risks for the benefit of those around me. I hoped my deep care for the team would shine through. I loved every job I'd ever had and was fascinated with how generating wealth could create more opportunities, provide for more people, and make dreams come true during this season. I often reminded myself of the belief that through leading with values at the forefront and making one wise decision after another, we could build something special.

The Gift of Humility

In those early days, it was tempting to fake it by pretending like I knew more than I did. The one thing I did know was that if I tried to act like I had it all together, everyone would have called my bluff in a heartbeat. In hindsight, the sheer speed of the transition and lack of preparation would provide a distinct and unexpected advantage. Instead of pretending I knew everything about the business, I had little choice but to embrace *humility*.

Humility is often misunderstood as a low self-regard or simply as the opposite of pride. However, in leading a team over the years, I've learned that **humility is better defined as an *accurate view of one's strengths and weaknesses.*** After all, it's far less important for a leader to excel at everything and far better to know where our strengths end, where our weaknesses begin, and where we have room for growth. In a time when imposter syndrome plagues so many leaders with fear, doubt, and insecurity, true *humility* can be as effective of a cure as anything I know.

In many facets it felt like *humility* was thrust on me by my circumstances and ignorance, but it was integral in shaping my life as a young leader and helped set a foundation for creating a healthy team culture in four significant ways:

1. Openly Acknowledging My Weaknesses

Humility invited me into openly acknowledging my lack of experience. I knew I had a lot to learn, and I certainly didn't want to be the "emperor with no clothes." So, instead of hiding what I didn't know, I decided to be transparent about it. Having not seen a P&L or cash flow statement for the business, it was far better to ask our VP of finance to walk me through the financial statements than to pretend I knew it all in public and be forced to pick it up on my own in private. Being honest about my limitations garnered support, deepened connection with the team, and reduced the burden of having to know all the answers from the get-go. When leaders aren't willing to acknowledge their limits and instead prop themselves up as know-it-alls, it can lead people to focus on highlighting their leader's weaknesses rather than protecting them and offering support.

2. Admitting I Can't Do It on My Own

Humility helped me realize I couldn't do it all on my own. Rest assured, given the scope of the business and all I didn't know, trying to carry the load by myself would've been an utter failure. The leader who thinks they're the best at everything is inevitably the cowboy who ends up with a load too heavy to carry, while willing people watch and wait for instructions. As overwhelm sets in and pressure grows, it becomes even more difficult to slow down and invite others to work together in moving the organization forward.

3. Highlighting the Strengths of Others

Humility creates space to highlight the strengths of others. From balance sheets to interventional suites, pivot tables to MRI cables, the expertise within our team was and still is mind-boggling. A right-sized awareness of my limitations became a gateway to seeing and celebrating other people's strengths. *Humility* created space for everyone to shine. While my knowledge has increased and my strengths have grown over time, it's been a total blast to see members of the team learn, tackle, and accomplish things I'd never think to attempt, let alone succeed at, on my own.

4. Carrying a Growth-Oriented Mindset

Humility helped to keep me curious and to guide us toward a growth culture. Because of my lack of experience, we became a culture of question-askers. I can't count the number of times right out the gate that I had the privilege of looking at one of our leaders and asking, "What direction do you think we should head?" or "What would you do if you were in my shoes?" What a gift to everyone involved to have the opportunity to learn and invest in making decisions that would shape the company's future!

Humility Is Courageous

As we wrap up on *humility* and prepare to dive into the secret to flipping the Me-Cycle upside down, it's important to recognize that *humility* isn't passive, weak, or insecure—it's *courageous*. It takes tremendous strength of character to acknowledge what we don't know and shine a light on others' strengths. ***Humility* allows us to carry confidence even amid uncertainty and helps us to celebrate how far we've come while remaining resilient in what we've yet to learn.**

It's crazy to think about the gift that *humility* was to my twenty-nine-year-old self. Through inviting others to the leadership party, *humility* both created opportunity and lightened the leadership load. Looking back, I'm so grateful the team garnered up the trust to jump in with both feet. Once we found our footing post-transition, we would have the opportunity to shift our focus from surviving to thriving.

Tripping into Culture

Somewhere in the midst of being abruptly handed the leadership baton, a friend gifted me a copy of Patrick Lencioni's *The Five Dysfunctions of a Team*. To my embarrassment, I can't remember which friend it was; if it was you, please let me know, because that gift has had an immeasurable impact on my life, leadership, and the

Block Imaging story. From the moment I cracked open *The Five Dysfunctions of a Team*, the hope and handholds Lencioni provided served as water in the desert as I ventured into the great unknown of leading our family business.

For those who aren't familiar with Patrick Lencioni or the Table Group, I strongly recommend *The Motive*, *The Advantage*, *The Working Genius*, and *Getting Naked*. (Don't worry or get excited; it's about running good

meetings!) In all seriousness, Lencioni's insights not only opened my eyes to a fresh perspective on leadership but also expanded my horizons around creating a culture where both people *and* performance matter. And I'm proud to say that over the last decade, he's not only become a mentor but a friend. Okay, we may not be best friends just yet, but we did meet and take a photo together in San Francisco, so I'm convinced he thinks we're as close as I do. I just sit by the phone at night, waiting for him to call.

In the early pages of the book, before even making it to the five dysfunctions, there were two quotes that captured my attention and became lighthouses in the midst of the wind and waves of those early months at the helm: **"Not finance, not strategy, not technology. It is teamwork that remains the ultimate competitive advantage, both because it is so powerful and so rare."** Really? Teamwork is more critical than finance, strategy, or technology? That's a pretty bold assertion. But Lencioni doesn't stop there: **"If you could get all the people in an organization rowing in the same direction, you could dominate any industry, in any market, against any competition at any time."**[3]

Was he really saying that culture wasn't just key to creating a great place to work but was actually

---

[3] Patrick M. Lencioni, *The Five Dysfunctions of a Team: A Leadership Fable* (London: Jossey-Bass, 2002).

foundational to dominating in the marketplace? That was a super exciting meshing together of my passion for people and Block Imaging's deep need for strengthening performance. Talk about the right book at the right time.

These two quotes (or perhaps promises) resonated deep in my bones for two reasons. First, I knew our organization had become fragmented and definitely wasn't rowing in the same direction. In times of uncertainty, it's common for people to shift toward self-preservation—the antithesis of teamwork. Second, these insights offered hope to a young leader passionate about business and people but with a limited background in the technical facets of the role. In the midst of the unknown, I found great comfort in the idea that organizational health could be the ticket to success both in shaping culture and driving performance.

Leading up to my transition, while I was still responsible for sales in the Midwest, my understanding of the larger organization was beyond limited. I could distinguish between a CT scanner and an MRI, but I had no experience with our office in Tokyo, and like I said, I was woefully blind to the financial nuts and bolts of the larger organization. Faced with the enormity of what I didn't know, teamwork as *the* ultimate competitive advantage sounded like a pretty compelling and tangible starting point for moving the company forward.

But it wasn't simply the concept of teamwork that drew me in; it was the premise that through cultivating a healthy culture, we'd achieve *uncommon* results *through* getting better *by* working together. Perhaps instead of building an organization filled with politics, toxicity, ego, manipulation, and a vast disconnect between the management and staff that plague so many office cultures, creating a place where people work together in healthy ways could change the game in the way people view and approach work. Maybe, just maybe, Lencioni's insights about organizational health and culture were the keys to closing the gap between my own experiences and the world's view of work.

So, with little time to prepare and no choice but to show up and grow up, I took Pat at his word, hoped he was right, and pushed all in toward fostering a healthy team culture.

While cultural transformation doesn't happen overnight, as I reflect on our commitment to create a place where people matter fifteen years later, imperfect as we are, I'm amazed at how far we've come. I'm blown away by how our team of more than four hundred cares so deeply for one another and the healthcare community we serve. And, lest culture get pegged as the "ooey gooey, touchy feely" stuff, it's important to share that teamwork has not only been better for the team but has also led to some pretty remarkable results in terms of revenue and profitability since the journey began.

"Good for you, Josh. Great story. But how do *I* do it?"

We're getting there. Stick with me while we take a quick minute to bring some context to culture ahead of diving into the three T's that flip the Me-Cycle upside down.

Level Up

Humility is leading with a clear understanding of your strengths and weaknesses. It helps leaders grow and create environments in which others can thrive. Take a moment to reflect on these questions:

- Where do my strengths shine when it comes to leading people?
- What's an area that tends to trip me up as a leader?
- What's one thing I could lean into to help close the gap between where I am now and where I want to be?

Keeping It Real

Mackenzie
Technical Support Lead | 8 years at Block

People matter first came alive for me when I realized, early in my Block career, that my leader Micah genuinely cared about me not just as an employee but as a person. He wasn't being kind to get something out of me. He was kind because he truly cared about my well-being. That sincerity inspired me to grow—both in my role and as a person.

I've seen the three T's—*together*, *thoughtful*, and *transparent*—play out most clearly in how communication is handled. Decisions here are made with care, then shared openly and clearly. Even when something is already decided, leadership still invites the team into the conversation. Questions are encouraged, context is offered, and buy-in is pursued so we can move forward together, not just follow along.

One moment I'll never forget was a tough conversation I had with Josh. I disagreed with him on an emotional topic, and I was digging in hard. He responded with grace and patience in the moment and then circled back afterward to debrief. He gave me feedback on how I might handle future hard conversations with more clarity and then asked for feedback in return: How did I feel in the moment? How did I perceive *his* approach? That moment made me feel incredibly safe and seen. I was allowed to disagree, even emotionally, and I was still treated with respect and curiosity. We both got better because of it.

Over the years, my leadership support has grown in big ways. I've been working closely with our VP of communications, Amy, on developing as a leader, and it's been transformational. I've learned how to ask for what I need at work and in my personal life. I've learned to approach conflict with curiosity rather than fear.

This is not a perfect company. We don't pretend to be. But when something goes wrong—whether it's a project, a plan, or something in your personal life—you're never left alone. There's always support. I've met some of my best friends at Block, and being part of this team feels like being part of a family.

To me, *People Matter at Work* is about being holistic. When we say someone matters *at work*, we're really saying they matter *everywhere*. The line between personal and professional life is thinner than ever. Block understands that when you help someone grow at work, you're helping them grow at home too.

Trevor

Director of Technical Excellence | 4 years at Block

There were two moments early on when *people matter* came alive for me. The first was right after I accepted the role and began preparing to move across the country from Colorado. The project management team sent audiobook recommendations for the drive. It was such a small gesture but it meant a lot. It showed they were thinking about me even before I walked through the doors.

The second moment came when two team members, Emberly and Kylie, sent a personalized list of local school districts, doctors, dentists, daycare centers—all the practical things you forget to think about when you're relocating. That kind of thoughtfulness made us feel truly cared for as we started over in a new place.

Since then, I've seen the three T's—*together, thoughtful,* and *transparent*—lived out regularly. My leader, Micah, has modeled them consistently. I believe he learned that from those who led him, and in turn, he's led me the same way. And now, I feel called to carry that forward with those I lead.

One moment I'll never forget was when we lost a team member. Josh personally came to our tech-ex team, gathered us together, and shared the news with us. It was leadership at the deepest and most human level. Several teammates told me later how that moment changed the way they viewed Block because of Josh's willingness to show up personally, slow down, and show care in that moment.

Before Block, I never felt empowered in my professional life. Now, I feel trusted to lead not just at work but in my personal life as well. I've grown in confidence, wisdom, and clarity, and that's been the result of being taught, led, and trusted. And because I've experienced that, I'm driven to give it away to others.

People matter is the centerpiece. It's not just a slogan; it's a daily practice.

If I had to summarize it in two words: *Love well*. To see people fully in the midst of all of their challenges and shortcomings, but also their strengths. To always be asking, "How can we love them well, so they're equipped, encouraged, and empowered in everything they do at work and in life?" That's what *People Matter at Work* means to me.

CHAPTER 3

Revealing the Heart of Culture

As Tolstoy famously wrote in *Anna Karenina*, "All happy families are alike; each unhappy family is unhappy in its own way." So it is with organizations great and small. For that reason, flipping the Me-Cycle requires some clarity and intention. Here's a set of ten questions to help us put a finger on the pulse of a workplace's culture. Take a moment to score (either for the team you lead or the entire organization) each question with 1 for Yes, 2 for Kinda, and 3 for No:

- Do people trust their fellow teammates?
- Do people trust their leadership?
- Does the team hold itself to high standards?

- Are people energized and fulfilled by their work?
- Do team members enjoy their fellow team members and laugh together?
- Do meetings have a clear purpose and steps to take at the end?
- Do team members feel safe to speak up when they disagree?
- Do most people go home feeling invested in?
- Do people carry a deep sense of ownership?
- Do customers like working with your organization?

Alright, let's tally up. If you scored between 10 and 15, congratulations because you're at a great starting point. If you scored between 16 and 22, there's a blend of potential and concern. If the 3's were popping in your head like popcorn . . . I'd venture to guess that each day feels like a new roller coaster that you can't wait to end. If you found yourself between 23 and 30, it's probably a great time to ask whether you have the influence and stamina to be part of the solution or if it's time to find a healthier place to immerse yourself.

Regardless of whether the current landscape is positive and the culture is healthy, or if toxicity, politics, and negativity feel ever present, I hope that the stories and handholds in the chapters that follow will be catalytic in closing the gap between where the team is today and where you'd hope it to be in the years to come.

The Air We Breathe

Over the years, I've had the opportunity to work with countless leaders within the healthcare space and across all sorts of other industries as they've sought to learn more about the "secret sauce" to creating a healthy culture. Whether I'm speaking with the leader of a family business where the owners are at odds or a regional vice president who feels overworked and underappreciated in a Fortune 500 company, I can't help but notice the comparison between culture and air quality.

For the average person in a place with decent air quality, unless you're snorkeling, exercising, or smoking a pipe, we rarely think about breathing. We subconsciously exchange stale carbon dioxide for fresh oxygen. All day and all night. *Inhale. Exhale. Inhale. Exhale.*

While the realities of a culture may be less physically evident, the workplace culture we're part of is as impactful on people's lives as the air we breathe. Imagine for a moment being part of the optimal meeting scenario: There's a clear agenda, the right people are present, the conversation flows smoothly, and the meeting ends a few minutes early.

If your leader or team is prone to long and laborious meetings without much direction, you might be thinking: "Alright, Josh, you're really stretching it now."

Stick with me for just a minute! Imagine we're in a beautiful conference room on the twenty-third floor, overlooking Camelback Mountain in Phoenix. The lighting and temperature are perfect, the A/V equipment functions flawlessly, and the space is free from distractions. The environment is prime for connection, creativity, and productivity. What a meeting!

Now, let's hop into the elevator and head down to the basement. The elevator doors open, and we see . . . nothing. It's so dark that it's hard to tell how big the room is. The temperature is a chilling 58 degrees, and even the most technical person in the room can't get the slide deck pulled up or the remote team members connected. Just as the meeting is about to start, smoke begins to billow in from under the double doors in the corner. Within seconds, the fire alarms blare. The air thickens. People's eyes start to water as they try to find the fastest way to escape.

If you're like me, you can feel your breath quickening just by imagining this atmosphere; now imagine living in it for two thousand hours a year. The thought of a smoke-filled basement triggers a shift from *thriving* to *surviving*, all without even being in the space.

The difference between a healthy and toxic culture is unmistakable. In healthy environments, people trust one another, sharpen ideas through collaboration, take ownership, and bring their best because they feel safe and valued. In toxic cultures, trust breaks down. People hold back, play it safe, avoid risks, and retreat into isolation—not because they don't care but because the environment tells them it's not worth the cost. What are the "smoke signals" of an unhealthy culture? Blaming, shaming, and gaming.

Blaming: Instead of taking responsibility for attitudes, actions, or outcomes, it's always someone else's fault.

Shaming: Instead of honoring people's effort and investment, the focus is on problems and the fact that no one is smart enough or working hard enough to satisfy the boss.

Gaming: In unhealthy companies, people spend most of their time and energy battling themselves rather than focusing their attention toward serving customers and battling the competition.

What Is Culture, Really?

Culture is one of those terms that can mean everything and nothing at the same time. Unfortunately, for lots of leaders and organizations, culture is often

1. diminished as "soft stuff,"
2. viewed as a creative way to manipulate people into feeling good about giving more,
3. relegated to HR, or
4. seen as something that's formed by happenstance versus something we build.

Before we dive into the secret sauce of a healthy culture, let's take a moment to explore what culture *really* is and why it's the heartbeat of every organization.

Merriam-Webster defines culture in the workplace setting as "the shared attitudes, values, goals, and practices that characterize an institution or organization." The culture we foster is a reflection of every action and interaction that takes place in our organizations; the same applies to our families, and like our families, the layers are deep and evolving. It's often way easier to feel the culture of a place or group than to describe it, and it's most certainly easier to verbally espouse its merits than to intentionally shape it. That being said, like gravity, **culture will exert an indelible impact on everyone within its reach, regardless of their belief in its existence or significance.**

The reality is while I hear the significance of culture talked about a ton, for most leaders culture is something we just live with. **Many mistakenly believe it surrounds us like the weather, and the only way to change it is to move somewhere else.** As we see in the Me-Cycle and will see shortly in the We-Cycle, **it is foundational that the leader gets the ball rolling through the *establishment* and *embodiment* of the values they hope to perpetuate throughout their organization.**

Backpacks on Fire

In 2020, our new director of marketing (and now VP of communications), Amy, shared an amusing and thought-provoking story. She joined Block Imaging a couple of months into the COVID-19 pandemic. About six months later, her husband picked her up after work because her car was in the shop. Expecting the usual "How was your day?" routine, she was surprised when he instead commented on the contrast between the way people left the building at Block compared to her previous employer.

At her last job, he said, people rushed out of the building at the end of the day "like their backpacks were on fire." But in his couple of minutes waiting at Block, he noticed that people trickled out slowly, engaging in conversations, leaning on cars, and even exchanging hugs before departing. Whether it was just a beautiful day or close friends saying goodbye, the cultural difference was striking enough for him (a relative outsider) to take notice. While I would've never equated the health of a culture with how people physically leave the office at the end of the day, it's a reminder that **the impact of a strong and healthy team culture is as surprising and enduring as the quality of the air we breathe.**

Chick-fil-A Versus McDonald's

Recently, I ran into a young entrepreneur named TJ at a high school volleyball game featuring his sister and my daughter. TJ had been a summer intern at Block Imaging years back, and we had stayed in touch as he started a couple of car washes and Zed's ice cream in

Austin, Texas. In between points, TJ served up the question of a lifetime:

"Josh, do you really think culture is that important?"

Though phrased as a question, I couldn't help but sense a hint of cynicism.

I thought to myself, "Is he seriously asking this?" I mean, TJ job-shadowed with me during college. He knows how big of a deal this is in my life and in our organization. As I gathered my thoughts, my mind raced through a decade of studying and practicing company culture, preparing to launch a full defense. Instead, a light bulb went off in my head, and I volleyed back a question of my own.

"TJ, let me ask you something. Is there a difference between Chick-fil-A and McDonald's?"

His posture shifted instantly. Without hesitation he responded, "Hell, yeah, there's a difference!"

What made him respond like that? What's the big deal? After all, it's just fast food, right? Sure, I have 21,000 points in my Chick-fil-A app, but it's just chicken, waffle fries, and shakes—right?

In lots of ways, these two chains are similar. Both have thousands of locations, serve fast food, sport highly recognizable logos, and have meaningful core values plastered on their walls. Yet, despite their similarities, the differences couldn't be more stark. Some might even say that Chick-fil-A has a cult(ure) following. You can literally feel the difference before you enter the parking lot (with the inevitable line of cars wrapped around the corner at all hours of the day).

Not only is Chick-fil-A recognized as one of the top companies to work for nationally, but the impact of that healthy culture trickles down to everything, including hiring, retention, customer satisfaction, and, notably, same-store sales, which are more than double those of McDonald's. Suffice it to say, yes TJ, it's "my pleasure" to share about the significance of culture as it relates to both people and performance.

The Conundrum of Creating Culture

This is where it gets really fun. As leaders, we have the privilege of elevating and embodying the values and behaviors that will define what's normal, and we get to invite others to help shape the culture we're striving to build. Whether you're the apex leader responsible for leading the charge across the entire organization or a team leader whose circle of influence lies in a specific area or department, you get to decide the kind of culture you want to create.

Over time, the culture we foster will reflect what we value and how we relate to and set expectations for others. **We will perpetuate what we celebrate**, and Andy Stanley, author and host of *The Andy Stanley Leadership Podcast*, is spot-on when he says, **"We will**

become what we're willing to tolerate." If we allow for people to dishonor one another and provide a poor customer experience, we will in time reside in a culture filled with those behaviors. The exciting part is, whether you know it or not, *you already have a vision for the culture you want to create.* Because our values flow from our beliefs, and our actions align with our beliefs 100 percent of the time (give or take a little human error, acknowledged with *humility*), it's often just a matter of taking the time to unearth, communicate, and embody that vision to the people in your care.

At Block, flowing out of my belief that *people matter* more, it's important for me to be a leader who carries honor for people. And guess what one of our Block Imaging values is today? *Honor.* Our other values—*together, integrity, growth*—rest on top of our mission and give shape to our organizational identity. As you'll see later in the book, these aren't just nice words that hang on a wall, but on our best days, they guide and can be felt in every decision we make, large and small. Quite frankly, letting our values lead the way makes decision-making far easier and way more fun.

I love what John Maxwell says in *The 21 Irrefutable Laws of Leadership*: "The speed of the leader is the speed of the team."[4]

---

[4] John Maxwell, *The 21 Irrefutable Laws of Leadership: Follow Them and People Will Follow You* (Nashville: Thomas Nelson, 1998).

While I certainly believe it's true, I've seen it expand far beyond speed. The reality is you can fill in the blank: "The _____ of the leader is (or will in time become) the _____ of the team." Attitude, effort, generosity, kindness, ambition, gossip, love . . . whether we realize it or not, our culture will eventually form around what the leaders value and live out. Over time, teams will adopt and mirror the values and tendencies of their leaders, which is why it's so crucial for us as leaders to be aware of our influence. As a leader, you may not always choose the values on the organization's website, but you *do* get to choose what actions will be commonplace and those that won't be tolerated in the team you lead. For those who aspire to lead, this is an incredible time to begin creating a future vision for the culture you hope to create and the leader you need to become in pursuit of shaping such a culture.

Culture or Behavior: Which Comes First?

Whether culture or behavior comes first is the age-old chicken-and-egg debate. Which one precedes and gives way to the other? I love how James Clear, author of *Atomic Habits*, ties habits, behaviors, and culture together: **"One of the most effective things you can do to build better habits is to join a culture where your desired behavior is the normal behavior."** He goes on to say, "The normal behavior of a tribe often overpowers the desired behavior of the individual."[5]

Whoa.

In other words, **values guide actions, actions shape culture, culture informs behavior, behavior reinforces culture, and the culture we're a part of strengthens our values.** As leaders and culture-shapers, that's ultimately what we're striving for—to create an environment where healthy behaviors become contagious and, well, normal! For some, the key is to move beyond merely complaining about and perpetuating the negative culture we're in and to begin *dreaming* about the culture we want to be a part of, *embodying* the behaviors that we want to be prevalent, and *communicating* to those we lead what we're after and why it's so important!

Simon Sinek sums it up perfectly: **"Leaders set the culture. Leaders are responsible for overseeing the environment in which people are asked to work . . . and the people will act in accordance with that culture."** This couldn't be more true. Setting the culture is one of our most important responsibilities as leaders. It's tempting to focus most of our time and energy on

---

[5] James Clear, *Atomic Habits: An Easy & Proven Way to Build Good Habits & Break Bad Ones* (New York: Avery, 2018).

what Lencioni refers to as the "smarts" side of the coin—finance, strategy, product development, and customer service. While these aspects are important too, they're best achieved when people are operating within a strong, healthy, and vibrant team culture.

A Question-Asking Culture

Growing up and into my adult years before ever stepping into the role of president, I frequently asked my dad all sorts of questions about the business. While many found his strong presence intimidating, I loved understanding his thought process and his "why" behind decisions. Whether it was about our 401(k) plan, sales techniques, or business strategy, I'd ask questions and he'd answer them. Looking back, I realize that asking bold questions was an incredible way to gain context. And with more context came even better questions.

That brings me back to "the _____ of the leader is the _____ of the team." Today, question-asking is a core part of our organizational DNA at Block Imaging. Every company-wide meeting and Block U onboarding course starts with a slide stating that we are a "question-asking culture" and ends with an open Q&A. In other words, something instrumental to my development has become a central part of how we roll as a team.

Culture Affects Everything and Everyone

One of my absolute favorite aspects of creating a workplace where people thrive is the positive impact it has on their families and, in particular, how it helps shape their children's view of work. Let's compare how two people return home at the end of the day.

Employee #1 comes home discouraged. Their name isn't that important since, deep down, they're just a number to the boss. They don't work out of their strengths or seem to make much of a difference. Their boss vacillates between being distant and unavailable or nitpicking the smallest details. They don't feel like they have much of a voice, and the unspoken message is "Just stay in your lane and do what needs to be done."

On the other side of the coin, we have James. James comes home energized after working alongside his tech-support team to navigate two challenging service situations. Toward the end of the day, James was able to help the engineer get the first system up and running, and he's confident the parts that are scheduled to arrive in the morning will allow the second site to resume scanning patients by lunch. James worked within his strengths, and his leader encouraged him along the way with a mix of autonomy and direction. He was free to be creative in finding more efficient solutions and learned a couple of new things throughout the day. After a challenging day, he went home grateful for the part he got to play in serving the team, supporting customers, and ultimately impacting patient care.

Now, imagine extending these scenarios over weeks, months, and years. What's the tangible difference when these people walk through their front doors and greet their families or roommates? From dinners and diapers to dance recitals and doctor's appointments, the culture we're a part of for over two thousand hours a year has a significant impact on homes, families, and communities. Looking back all these years later, one of the best litmus tests and greatest rewards of creating a vibrant culture is hearing a story about a son or daughter who tells their parents they want to work at a place someday like where their mommy or daddy works.

At the end of the day, the culture we foster will have an impact on *everything* that happens and *everyone* who comes in contact with our organization. Because the ripples are inevitable, our shaping ought not to be accidental but pursued with deep intention.

Level Up

Now that we've explored the importance of culture, let's start with the end in mind by exploring the future impact you want to have on the people you lead.

- How do you want people to feel when they go home at the end of the day?

- What do you want to be true of the people who are part of your team for five years?
- What characteristic, attitude, or behavior do you want to be more true of your team in twelve months?
- What characteristic, attitude, or behavior is having a negative effect and you'd like to see it reduced by 50 percent in the next twelve months?

Keeping It Real

Amy
Vice President of Communications | 5 years at Block

There were several moments early in my onboarding that began to reveal that *people matter* wasn't just a phrase at Block—it was something real. One of the first came when Josh texted me the day he knew I was leaving my previous job. He didn't ask about logistics or start dates. He just checked in, knowing it might be an emotional day, and genuinely wanted to know how I was doing.

But the moment I knew for sure was when a new team member I had brought in shared a personal dream: He wanted to change the spelling of his name to better reflect who he truly was. But the cost was just out of reach. Without hesitation, Josh made sure that money wasn't an obstacle. No production. No announcement. Just care. That moment was a tangible example that people here are seen as *whole* people, not just employees. Leaders at Block care how you're doing in every area of life because they understand that overall well-being affects how we show up for our team, our customers, and our families.

One of the clearest reflections of this culture comes during our annual retreat. Sitting in the conference room just before we kick things off is my favorite moment of the year. Unlike events at other companies where excitement is rare, and participation feels obligatory, our retreat is something the entire team looks forward to. It's a space where people are genuinely present and eager to learn, reconnect, and recharge our collective commitment. Helping to plan that day has been one of my proudest professional accomplishments.

Before Block, I spent a lot of time in self-protection mode. Not because I wanted to but because I had to just to survive. I learned to keep my guard up, to replay interactions, and to always assume there might be an ulterior motive. That posture bled beyond work into my personal life, especially as I entered motherhood—something that, in many organizations, is still seen as a liability for a woman trying to build a career.

My time at Block has been healing. Slowly, I learned that this is a safe place to be myself. I don't need to overanalyze every email or second-guess every question. And on the days I do start to spiral, I have enough evidence to remind myself, "That's not how it works here."

I've learned to lead with trust. To be more open and vulnerable. To say, "I don't know the answer," or "Can we reschedule? I'll be on a field trip with my child," or even "I'm walking through a hard season with my family." It takes time to unlearn those defensive habits—but I'm growing.

This culture isn't smoke and mirrors. It's real. It pushes you to evolve and become a better version of yourself. If you're looking for a job where you can punch a clock and coast, this probably isn't the place. But if you want to grow, be challenged, and be *seen*, it's a rare and beautiful fit.

At the heart of it all is *trust*. I'm trusted to do my job well. I trust the people around me. And I trust that our leadership is equipped and committed to doing what's best for this team. That kind of trust doesn't just sit at the top; it flows through the entire organization.

Ben

Parts Harvest Manager | 11 years at Block

Before I ever worked at Block, I kept hearing buzz about the culture from friends in our community. I didn't know exactly what that meant at the time, but I knew I wanted to be part of it.

I clearly experienced the three T's—*together, thoughtful,* and *transparent*—during the COVID pandemic. While friends and family described fear and isolation at their workplaces, my experience was completely different. We had weekly town halls just to process what was happening. We had no agenda, just space to ask questions and navigate that season together. There was honesty, vulnerability, and a lot of thoughtfulness in how leadership navigated that time. Those were defining moments, and we didn't avoid them: We leaned in.

One of the things that's impacted me most, though, is how far *together* extends. It's not just about the people who clock in each day. Block has embraced my family in a way I never expected. Having Josh, Jason, and countless others genuinely invest in the lives of my wife, Tracee, and my son, Bellamy, it's hard to describe how meaningful that is. It's a gift. And it's helped me realize that when we say *people matter*, we're not just talking about the team; we're talking about the people we *love* too.

Anytime someone close to me complains about their job, I can't help but think, "Man, I have it so good." Block has given me room to grow in my role and in the responsibility I've been entrusted with. Before this, I had dropped out of college and was selling skateboards. I never imagined I'd be looking forward to the kind of future I now see ahead.

But here's the thing, you've got to *want* this kind of culture. You can try it on for size, but if it doesn't line up with what you value, it might not feel like home. I can tell you all the ways Block has impacted my life, my family, and my future. But that impact happens only if you're looking for what this culture is rooted in.

If I had to sum it up, I'd say the *people matter* culture at Block is born from love—real love. That's what makes it different. And that's what makes it worth being part of.

PART II

The Three T's

The moment has arrived. Now that we've laid the groundwork for how we got here, introduced our culprit (the Me-Cycle), and highlighted the power of humility and the significance of culture, this is where the rubber meets the road. In the pages that follow, you'll find the heartfelt and hard-fought wisdom discovered over fifteen years of chasing after a workplace culture where people thrive and everyone wins.

As a refresher, in the simplest form of the Me-Cycle, bosses look out for themselves and focus primarily on what they can take from their employees. This leads to people feeling like objects. Far too frequently, they return the favor by primarily focusing on themselves and what they can get out of the organization and, worse, their colleagues.

Everything changes when *me* turns to *we*. **In the We-Cycle, bosses become leaders—the kind of leaders who care more about the people they lead than the position they hold.** It's not that power, position, prestige, and pay don't become part of the leadership equation; it's just that they become more of an outcome than a pursuit. **In the We-Cycle, employees become team members—team members who row alongside the leader in moving the organization forward.** These aren't mere word shifts or linguistic changes. They're mindsets that ultimately become identities that change everything for everyone.

In the chapters ahead, we're going to dig into the three T's that revealed themselves along the way as we sought to flip the Me-Cycle upside down. When my title

THE THREE T'S

changed overnight in 2011, it's no surprise that the culture didn't. But a hope would become a vision, and a vision would eventually manifest itself through leading with the three T's. They would become crucial to guiding the attitudes and actions that started the engine of the We-Cycle at Block Imaging. That engine would drive us toward creating the thriving team and high-performance culture we're known for today.

Keeping It Real

James

Account Executive | 1 year at Block

People matter came alive for me the moment I walked through the door. I've worked in plenty of soulless offices, but there's something different here, something tangible. Within the walls of Block Imaging, there's a sense of peace and belonging that's hard to describe but easy to feel.

As an account executive in the field, I see the three T's—*together, thoughtful,* and *transparent*—play out all the time. Recently, we had to modify a C-arm rental agreement. Instead of hiding behind emails or making a unilateral decision, our product manager and I met with the customer face-to-face. We explained the situation with clarity, listened to their concerns, and worked together to find a solution. That kind of collaboration isn't just good for business; it's what trust looks like in action.

There's also a unique care for people that shows up in unexpected ways. I've received surprise postcards, Block-branded gear, and personal notes recognizing milestones such as celebrating ten thousand customer contacts. When someone on the team makes their first sale, our leader organizes a virtual lunch to mark the moment. It's not just acknowledgment—it's genuine celebration, and it motivates us to keep pushing forward *together*.

Working here has helped refine my communication skills in ways I didn't expect. I've learned to ask better questions that uncover the real challenges our customers face and point us to solutions that truly help. Better questions always lead to better outcomes.

What makes Block Imaging stand out most is its caring, family-like culture. From the CEO to the cleaning staff, people are treated with dignity and seen as people who matter. That foundation creates a positive, focused environment where we can do great work without unnecessary distractions.

In fact, the culture is what brought me back seventeen years after my first experience with Block. It left a mark the first time, and now I get to be part of it again.

What I see around me are people who work hard not just for themselves and their families but for the greater good of the team and the mission. Selfish teams don't last. But selfless teams? They go the distance. We're here to win, and we're here to win *together*. And when we do, those banners fly forever.

CHAPTER 4

Better *Together*

> If you want to go fast, go alone. If you want to go far, go *together*.
>
> —African proverb

In those early days after transitioning from sales rep to president, humility served as the ultimate flashlight in guiding us toward the first of the three T's: *Together*. While *together* can come in many forms as it relates to creating a culture with *people matter* at the forefront, let's define *together* as **collaborating to sharpen any decision of consequence.**

Carrying a *together* mindset wasn't just a cute platitude or hypothetical philosophy. It began as a straight-up lifeline, and to this day, it remains foundational to the decision-making process across our organization.

"What would you do if you were in my shoes?"

"What do you recommend we do in this situation?" Wash, rinse, repeat.

By following this simple pattern of *asking others for advice*, three significant outcomes naturally occurred:

1. I learned a ton.
2. The team's sense of ownership grew.
3. We made *way* better decisions.

What more could I ask for? It was like a cheat code.

"Sure, Josh," you say. "*Together* sounds great, but what does that look like, practically speaking, from a day-to-day perspective? I've got a business to run here."

For some leaders, it's natural to think that *together* is reserved solely for the big decisions, or when they have no clue what to do or are perhaps looking for some added confidence to validate their hunch. There are a host of reasons why leaders choose to make decisions in a silo instead of doing it *together*. For one leader, they think they're too busy to slow down and bring advisers in. For another, whether it be imposter syndrome or an authority complex, asking for help makes them feel weak or incompetent. And on the opposite end of the spectrum, some leaders are afraid to invite others into the decision-making process because they don't want to feel handcuffed by people's opinions or cause disappointment when they choose to move in a different direction. There are all sorts of reasons *not* to do it *together*, but the impact of bringing in others (inside and outside the organization) with more experience or a fresh perspective has been unquantifiable in shaping our culture and championing our success.

Hiring *Together*: The Story of Emily

One of my first and favorite times tripping into making a decision *together* was just a few months after moving to Lansing. This is a perfect example of what might have felt like a medium-sized decision at the time, and yet looking back, it's had a far greater impact than I could have imagined. Shortly after moving in 2011, I was looking to hire a sales support specialist. Another member of the team recommended Emily Jones because they thought we'd work well *together*.

Emily was a single mom at the time, looking to reenter the workforce. On the day of her interview, she was recovering from a cold and sounded like she'd been smoking Camel Reds for decades. After interviewing her for a bit, I remember thinking that while she seemed friendly and capable, with my lack of experience and her limited résumé, how could I be certain she was going to be a great fit for the role or the team?

Not entirely sure what to do next, I paused the interview and stepped out of the conference room for a moment. Three members of the team happened to be chatting nearby, so I brought them up to speed and asked if they'd be willing to spend some time with Emily right then and there and provide feedback on whether they thought we should hire her for the role. We were a much smaller organization at the time. Looking back, it sounds a little crazy and even unprofessional—throwing a definite curveball for Emily—but sometimes our values take the wheel and override conventional wisdom. After spending thirty minutes *together* with Emily, the impromptu interview panel said they thought she'd be a great fit. It might sound simple now, but it was one of those pivotal moments that began teaching me the power of making decisions *together*.

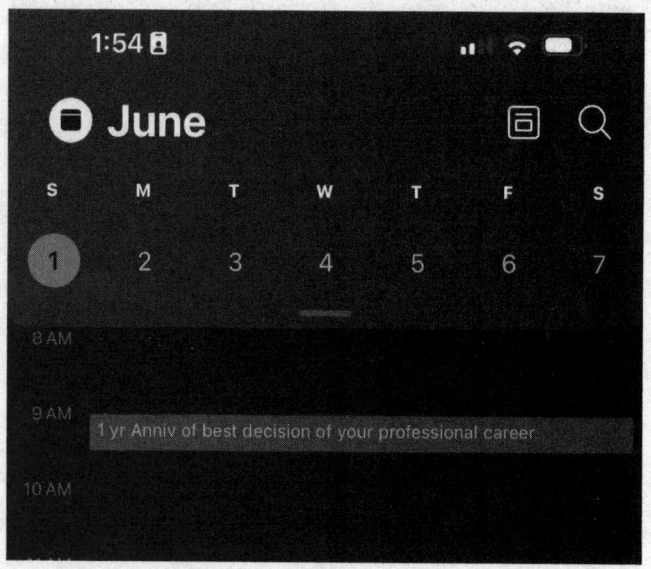

In following their advice, I made one of the best hires of my career. How could I forget it with this annual reminder (which Emily placed on my calendar all those years ago)?

As I shared earlier, Emily began as a sales support specialist, but just four months later she became my executive assistant, a role she would hold for the next twelve years. During that time, she gained experience and grew her leadership muscles. Over the years in her role as executive assistant, she played a crucial part in filling several leadership gaps. Then, in 2023, I encouraged her to take the leap into becoming our parts sales manager and eventually director of parts sales. Through raising six kids while battling cancer for the past seven years, Emily has embodied *people matter* in remarkable ways, and her impact on our organization is immeasurable. And it all started with a decision the team made by interviewing her *together*.

There is one last piece that's important to recognize. Asking others to join the interview process didn't just contribute to making a better decision; I also noticed that, after being part of the process, those team members carried an elevated sense of buy-in and were intentional in equipping, advocating for, and championing Emily as she started her new career. What began as a spontaneous *together* moment has evolved into a strategic part of our everyday hiring process to this day.

But Should We Hire Someone?

The value of making decisions *together* knows no bounds. It doesn't only impact decisions about who we should hire but can actually help determine whether we should hire a person in the first place. A few years back in our one-on-one meeting, our director of finance asked about expanding his team to address some capacity challenges in accounting. He was on the fence, so rather than simply answering, "Sure, Steve, whatever you think is needed to support the business," I encouraged him to pull his team *together* to share his thoughts and ask for their feedback.

"Josh, are you really saying you encouraged Steve to ask his team if they thought you should add someone else to the accounting department?"

Yup, that's right!

In a low-trust and low-ownership culture, it would be natural to assume that people will always say yes to hiring more help. After all, more people means less work, right? Not so fast.

Steve gathered his team to process the decision. After debating for a bit, they agreed that while there was a definite need to expand the team, they wanted to wait ninety days until the year-end review was complete so they could dedicate more time to the process of interviewing, onboarding, and training the new person.

At the end of the day, the power of *together* is far greater than simply making better decisions. In this situation, we not only made a more precise decision but the decision-making process communicated to the team that their voice mattered. After all, their awareness of the day-to-day workflow and the upcoming review provided a distinct advantage. Perhaps most important of all, by asking for their input, we acknowledged that the decisions we make carry an impact on their lives and work. In the end, when the amount of work felt overwhelming, rather than blame leadership for the lack of resources, the team was positioned to take responsibility, carry ownership, and ultimately learn as they watched the impact of their decision play out.

Global Leadership: *Together* from Afar

In March of 2011, shortly before I became president, the largest earthquake ever to hit Japan caused a tsunami that led to a nuclear disaster in Fukushima. In the months following the quake, our team in Tokyo was very afraid to travel around the country. Fast-forward to the next fall, in a unique confluence of circumstances, just a few weeks after my becoming president, our managing director in Japan brought a candidate to the table as a possible replacement for himself. I'll never forget standing in the only room in our home with good enough cell coverage as I spoke to the consulting firm we'd hired to help navigate operating in a country with a vastly different culture and business climate. Not only was there a ton of history and context I didn't know, but

I was literally talking to people who'd eaten breakfast on a day I'd yet to wake up to. Talk about feeling behind!

During this conversation, the consultants asked whether we intended to continue with the current managing director or hire the new candidate to lead the business forward. While the consulting firm recommended that we continue with the current director, there were a couple of pieces that led me to think otherwise.

Before the earthquake, we'd sent a project manager from the US to help act as a liaison between our Japan and US offices. Given the situation's complexity, I turned to the project manager, Megan, for advice. I explained the situation and shared that *we* had a decision to make. Did you catch that? Doing it *together* changed the operative word from *I* to *we*. Megan shared a few compelling reasons why she thought we should change directions and select the new candidate as the managing director going forward. Later that evening, I asked a few follow-up questions and made the call.

Megan's on-the-ground experience in Japan was crucial to making a wise decision; we would have been crazy not to recognize and appreciate her wisdom. Without her insight, I was flying blind and left with only my gut to trust. Instead, with a pinch of humility, a dose of submission, and three-fourths of a cup of *together*, the right decision all but made itself.

Co-Presidents Unite

As you will recall, in the early days of my transition, Jason Crawford was the president of Block Imaging Parts and Service, and I was president of Block Imaging International. In 2014, both businesses came under one roof at our new headquarters. We were so serious about leading *together* that even with numerous entities, Jason and I decided to shift and function as co-presidents. Two presidents? Yup. Eleven years later, with tons of growth and experience, there's not a consequential decision that hasn't been honed, shaped, or sharpened *together*.

When we're at our very best, Jason and I lead and embody *together*. As co-presidents, we've had the opportunity to submit to each other's strengths, protect each other's weaknesses, and quite literally show the organization what it looks like to work *together*. In a role that can be lonely and heavy at times, we get to carry the leadership load *together*.

Does this require *humility*? You bet it does. But that's the price of admission. It's worth it. In a time when ego and power often prevail within corporate structures, Jason and I leading side by side has been an invaluable gift to ourselves, each other, and the organization as a whole.

No Cowboys 'Round Here

In 2017, during the Q&A session at our annual company-wide retreat, a team member asked Jason and me about the most bothersome micro-behavior we saw in our organization. After hosting a lot of Q&A sessions over the years, there are often a number of possible answers that come to mind. But for some reason, this was one of those answers that felt like it was served up on a tee. Without hesitation, two words rose to the surface: *failing alone*.

At this stage in the journey, our team was better equipped and connected than ever before. We were in our twentieth year as a company, cell phones were now commonplace, and collectively our team had hundreds of years of experience completing thousands of transactions. Yet sometimes we'd still face situations in which decisions were made in isolation, leading to costly mistakes. It's one thing to make a poor decision. It's something entirely different to lose $50,000 because you were too independent, too impatient, or too arrogant to ask for help!

The price of acting like a lone cowboy is steep, so I pressed in a little further in answering the question: If we're going to fail, let's fail *together*. This was a turning point, and if the walls of Block Imaging could talk or you were to listen in on Teams calls throughout the day, you would hear people working *together* and deferring to one another in unique and dynamic ways. As the Navy

SEALs say, "Slow is smooth, smooth is fast." In cultures where *together* is practiced because trust is prevalent, people are far more likely to make smoother decisions that, believe it or not, lead to speed in the long run.

Poor Assessment

This just happened yesterday, so it's the freshest story in the book. Through the process of doubling in size over the last eighteen months, we'd let performance assessments fall off the radar as an organization. Our leaders weren't making time for them, and with so much going on in our HR space, we'd stopped holding people accountable for completing them for a bit. Because our best people want to know how they're doing and where they can grow, it was crucial for us to get back on track by ensuring one-on-ones and performance assessments were taking place across the organization.

Up to this point, we'd built a three-step process:

1. A team member performs a self-assessment.
2. The leader completes the team member's performance assessment.
3. The leader and team member get *together* to discuss what's been accomplished, where the team member has grown, and where they have the most opportunity to grow. Then they set growth goals for the future.

Given that the entire process revolves around step #1, I approached our leadership team with what I thought to be a simple and worthwhile idea for us to consider: "How about we drop the self-assessment to simplify and streamline the process and help get it back on track again?"

Let me just say the pushback was thorough and from all sides.

At first, I wrestled with the paradoxical nature of a team pushing back on the idea of simplifying something they weren't doing in the first place! Seriously?!? And yet, even though I didn't agree with their positions at first, it was important to remember that my end goal wasn't to change the process but to ensure that performance assessments were happening in a consistent and meaningful way. Over the next few minutes, leaders shared the merits of the self-assessment and the negative impact on the team of having one-sided assessments, especially after dropping the ball on the entire process for the past year.

In the end, the team not only recognized but emphasized the importance of the two-sided assessment process. By saying no to reducing the steps, they were saying yes to making them happen. This is a powerful example of what it looks like to highlight the vision and provide space for the team to work *together* on how that vision is implemented. It took some patience, humility, and flexibility, but in the end we had clarity and unity around this error being less about capacity and more about prioritization and discipline.

The Cost of Lone Leadership

One of the most common misconceptions about sharpening decisions *together* is that it'll take longer. After making thousands of decisions *together*, I've found the opposite to be true for at least two reasons.

The first is that leaders who make siloed decisions spend a ton of time explaining, defending, clarifying, and even cleaning up decisions on the backside. As my father-in-law once joked during a home renovation, "I cut it twice, and it's still too short." That carpentry phrase perfectly captures the cost of rushing ahead only to backtrack and need more materials. Moving fast and missing the mark is inefficient, costly, and ultimately harmful to the team.

The second reason lone leadership is ineffective is because it doesn't build capacity in others in the same way that making decisions *together* does. Sharpening decisions *together* is an incredibly powerful way to trade short-term speed for long-term efficiency by developing the people around us. After more than a decade of making decisions *together*, I believe it not only honors people and strengthens a culture but also serves to expand a leader's capacity in a way that dictating and passing down decisions to followers simply doesn't.

Balance: This Ain't No Democracy

Lone leadership is a real threat to team building, but the equal and opposite peril is looking for consensus in every decision. Let's be clear: Inviting input doesn't mean abdicating leadership or making decisions by committee or vote. Ultimately, as leaders, we're responsible for deciding who we ask to weigh in on a decision and then for making the final call.

Just this week, we had a situation arise that was sensitive in nature and complex in that it touched several different areas of the business. After hearing what had taken place, I reached out to the leader responsible for our service operations to hear his feedback. After discussing the issue, we brought our HR leaders up to speed. While I was anticipating going one direction, Micah, our VP of team culture, gave some valid reasons for taking a different course. Still not 100 percent sure, I reached out to Jason Crawford and a leader who'd just joined our team to get some fresh perspectives. I slept on the decision and changed my mind and began moving in the direction Micah had originally recommended . . . but it turned out more information came to light overnight that led to Micah changing *his* mind! He now felt like the original path I intended to take was the proper move. As we investigated further, *together*, the leader closest to the situation and I made the decision to go with Micah's original recommendation after all. In case you didn't catch all that: As more information came to light, both Micah and I changed our courses midstream, and I actually made the call to move forward with his initial recommendation.

While that situation was incredibly layered, the fact of the matter is there will inevitably be moments when we ask for advice but choose to move in a different direction. It's important to remember that we're asking people to *weigh in* on a decision, not *make* the decision. We're not abdicating responsibility. **Making the final call and owning the outcome remains in the hands of the leader.** That said, asking for input and inviting feedback in the decision-making process helps us make far better decisions as leaders and simultaneously elevates people's voices and their sense of ownership. Even when we move in a different direction than was recommended, if people feel genuinely heard, most team members will be appreciative of the opportunity to weigh in and will ultimately rally behind the decision.

One last note. While I'm not advocating decision by committee, if we find ourselves asking for input and consistently going in a different direction, it's probably a sign that we aren't asking the right people. Remember, when looking for help in strengthening a decision, it's vital to seek out the most knowledgeable people (inside or outside the organization) who are contextually in tune with the goals, values, and impact of the decision on the people, leader, and organization.

Much Bigger Than Work

In 2016, one of our team members lost their spouse to cancer shortly after giving birth to their third child. It was one of the most devastating experiences I've ever been a part of, both personally and professionally. I'll never forget visiting Mark and Nicole in the hospital as we joked about how flattering her compression socks were and how much she wanted to be home with her kids to make "dippy eggs" for their oldest son. Two weeks later, Nicole went into cardiac arrest and passed away at thirty-four. The grief was overwhelming, and the journey ahead for Mark and his three kids was unimaginable.

The funeral was both beautiful and heart-wrenching. There wasn't a dry eye as Mark courageously spoke about his bride. After the funeral, Lacey and I attended the graveside ceremony and watched as Mark stood alone as the casket was being lowered into the ground. People began making their way to their cars, and I remember feeling a strong urge to go stand by his side. While I may not have been his closest friend, Mark needed someone to be *together* with in that moment.

On that chilly spring day, my brother Jeremy and I flanked Mark on both sides for the longest half hour of my life with hardly a word spoken. I felt deeply ill-equipped and knew there was nothing I could say to ease his pain. However, it felt important that Mark knew he wasn't alone in his grief and that it was okay to stay in a moment that, once gone, could never be revisited. So we stayed until he was ready.

Looking back, it was one of the most sacred moments of my life. In the midst of the pain and grief, when it felt more natural to head to the cars with everyone else, my brother and I leaned into the opportunity to pause and be with Mark. In the hardest of times, it was a high honor to choose *together*.

While Nicole's passing was one of the most difficult stories I've ever encountered, it's crucial as leaders to be aware that the challenging situations going on in the lives of our team members are endless. While each person, story, and circumstance is different, it's a poignant reminder that *together* extends far beyond the walls of work and into people's lives and families. With *people matter* at the forefront, these tragic moments of showing up become less of a burden and more of a privilege and opportunity to come *together* and care deeply for people we lead.

You Don't Have To, You Get To

Whether it's making a decision or standing alongside a team member, we can look at *together* as something we "should do," but I think there's something far better in store for those who view it as something we "get to do." In my experience, with humility in mind, it is way more fun to make decisions *together*. When we get it right, we get to learn and celebrate; when we miss the mark, we get to learn and commiserate *together*.

Here's a quick look at the We-Cycle so far:

If you're someone who hasn't done this particularly well, I'd encourage you to sit down with a few people you work closely with and share openly that you want to be more intentional in asking better questions and leaning into their perspectives in decision-making. This gives them a heads-up and better prepares them for a new way of operating. If you want to make an incremental shift, I'd encourage you to begin practicing while it's fresh. "What do you think we should do here?" and "Which direction do you think we should head?" are a couple of great fire starters.

Level Up

Let's think about a couple of lenses to look through as we seek to embrace *together* in the days to come:

- Who can I invite to sharpen or strengthen this idea?
- Who will grow stronger because of the opportunity to see this decision play out from the early stages to the final result?
- Who on the team will be impacted, and who carries an outsized influence?

Now, let's move *together* to the second T as we seek to foster a thriving team culture.

Keeping It Real

Kevin
Director of Healthcare Solutions | 5 years at Block

Before joining Block, I came from a highly aggressive and competitive industry where culture was more of a slogan than a reality. We were pushed hard with little regard for our well-being and treated as revenue generators, not people. Our value was described like ripples in a bucket: Once gone, it was as if we were never there. That environment wore me down. It impacted my confidence and, eventually, my marriage.

From my very first weeks at Block, I experienced something radically different. My leader sent flowers to my wife and daughters while I was away on business to thank them for their sacrifice. In every 1:1, he created space to ask how my *family* was doing, not just how the *job* was going. That kind of care helped me rebuild both personally and professionally.

When I think about what stands out, it's how decision-making happens at Block. Even with decades of experience in the room, everyone gets a seat at the table. Leaders invite perspective, even from those with less tenure. The process of decision-making might look slower at first, but it's deliberate—because slow is smooth and smooth is fast.

The level of transparency here is second to none. I've watched financials, acquisitions, and major transitions be shared openly with the team. And while some may avoid calling a workplace a "family," I've felt it—during People Matter Days, in the way people are honored, and even in how many showed up at a recent funeral.

If I had to picture what Block feels like, I'd describe it like a soldier walking forward toward a goal with spear in hand, but no shield. Behind them stands a team, shields up, deflecting the arrows so the soldier can keep moving forward. That's what the leadership at Block does for us every day.

To me, *people matter* means focusing on the real needs of the people you lead. When that's done well, everything else falls into place.

Brandi
Parts Procurement Coordinator | 3 years at Block

I've seen *people matter* come alive through both heartache and celebration. I joined Block because of the people—and I was eager to dive into meaningful work. But life had other plans. A personal tragedy changed everything, pulling me into a journey I never expected. Through it all, I was met with kindness, understanding, and transparency. That experience and the way people showed up for me is why I'm still here. And I'm so thankful.

Over the past few years, I've experienced deep personal loss and faced the uncertainty that follows. In those seasons, I received more than sympathy. I received thoughtful feedback, handwritten notes, small gifts, and the steady support of a team that walked with me. One morning, I arrived to a message from a leader listing specific ways I had contributed to the team. I hadn't been looking for affirmation, but it hit me just how much I needed to hear those words.

At Block, we don't pretend to be perfect, but we pursue our values relentlessly. That's what creates a culture of courage and growth. I'm proud of how we call each other up when mindsets begin to drift toward fear or cynicism. "Fail Tales" during team meetings are one example. They normalize mistakes and remind us that failure isn't something to hide, but something to learn from. When I've made mistakes, I've never been met with shame or punishment, only the opportunity to own it, grow, and move forward.

This culture has given me room to build capacity, to stop comparing, and to lean into the strengths that make me uniquely valuable. I've developed a passion for leadership and a hunger for learning, something this team makes space for. Here, you can show up not knowing everything and be invited to grow anyway.

It's a team of possibility. If you're willing to show up, put in the work, pursue honest feedback, and maintain a growth mindset. It's a place where you can grow, learn, and become.

For me, trust is the foundation. It takes humility, time, and intention to build, and it can be lost in a moment. But when trust is valued, we fight for it. We repair it. We choose *we* over *me*. That's what *People Matter at Work* means: a relentless commitment to trust even when it's hard and a belief that people are always worth the effort.

CHAPTER 5

The Power of *Thoughtful* Decisions

As 2011 drew to a close, the mix of declining performance, Black Thursday, and the overnight change in leadership had stirred a deep sense of uncertainty. I knew the team and the leaders (many of whom were older and more experienced than me) were watching closely, as my approach in these early stages would set the tone for the "new normal." While it's a bit hard to explain where it originated, there was a word that resonated deeply and would become a true north for the season ahead. Over and over, there was a whisper inside that said:

"Josh, we just gotta be thoughtful in everything we do."

If *together* helped to get the engine started, being a *thoughtful* leader would get the steering wheel pointed in the right direction. While it might sound trite or elementary, this concept was a game changer as I sought to become a leader worth following and to create a culture where *people matter* most. I knew trust and stability wouldn't return overnight, but I hoped that working *together* to make one *thoughtful* decision at a time to regain momentum would get us moving in the right direction.

Defining Thoughtful

While the instinct to pursue *thoughtful* decisions came from a core conviction, in many ways it was simply in response to how I'd want to be led. After all, if I wanted to follow people who made *thoughtful* decisions, then it only made sense to be a leader who embodied the same. My goal was and is for the entire team, not just those in the room when decisions are made, to feel confident in our direction rather than being innocent bystanders to guess-and-go leadership. Over time, this commitment to being *thoughtful* in decisions and our care for the team in large and small ways has become a huge piece of creating a culture where people love to work and bring their best as a result.

In those early days after becoming president, the sheer number of decisions and their variety was stunning:

Should we add capacity to our HR team?

Does it make sense to begin distributing this new product?

Who should lead this area of the organization?

Should we consolidate two facilities into one?

What vendors should we consider for our new CRM?

Should we open an office in France?

How should we approach this upset customer?

What should we do about vacation time or maternity leave?

How should we handle performance assessments and compensation increases?

Even though I didn't have the answers on my own, it was my hope and expectation that by working *together*, we'd make solid, *thoughtful* decisions that would in turn rebuild trust, gain credibility, and invite people to jump in and move the ball forward.

Years after this principle and practice had become deeply embedded in our organization, I stumbled across a two-part definition of *thoughtful* that brought even deeper meaning. The first half is the idea of *showing careful consideration*.

"Wow, Josh, thanks a lot. That's deep. What kind of a leader doesn't do that?"

While it might seem obvious, let's not breeze past the importance of not just *carrying* careful consideration but *showing* careful consideration. No leader sets out to make thought*less* decisions, but it happens all the time. In fact, most of us have probably been on the receiving end of a poorly thought-out decision.

Whether we're talking about a big decision or a small one, it is a culture and morale killer when a leader makes a decision that can be quickly dismantled or that runs counter to the mission, values, or strategy of the organization. This sort of careless decision-making breaks trust and reduces confidence. While every decision isn't necessarily precedent-setting, each decision reflects what we value as leaders and not only shapes our reputation and culture but also serves to draw or repel people.

Now, for the mic drop part of the definition of *thoughtful*: "Showing careful consideration . . . ***for the needs of others***."

Take a moment to let that sink in. Though I didn't have this definition early on, it helped explain why the word *thoughtful* resonated so deeply in those early years. Showing careful consideration for the needs of others is such a powerful true north when it comes to flipping the Me-Cycle upside down and creating a place where people thrive at work. This second T is a great separator between a culture where employees are cogs in a wheel and a culture where *people matter* more. Making careful decisions is one thing, but considering the needs of those on the other side of the decision is a game changer. When decisions ignore people's needs or the impact each decision may have on them, the results can be devastating. And yes, we've learned this the hard way a few times . . .

No More Soda

Years ago, we made a big, sugary misstep—one that's still hard to forget. In an effort to tighten the reins on inter-company profitability, a couple of our leaders drew the conclusion that our engineering side of the business was losing money. To try and remedy this, one idea was to stem the tide by telling the team that they were no longer allowed to expense soft drinks when they were traveling.

You read that right. Block Imaging told our engineers who traveled the world installing and servicing medical equipment—many of whom spent more than one hundred nights a year in hotels—that the company couldn't afford (or didn't want) to buy them a soda with their dinner. It's a story that still makes me cringe to this day.

Now, think about the message that decision sent.

These engineers are critical to our mission and strategy. They arrange their own travel, order all sorts of expensive parts, and often work through the night to get vital systems up and running again so our customers and, most importantly, their patients don't miss out on life-changing scans. Our engineers are the face of the company to the customer, and we basically told them that their contribution wasn't worth the price of a Coke.

When I ask a room full of people at a speaking engagement if their leaders have ever made a thoughtless decision that had a significantly negative effect on the way they accomplish their work, it's common for more than 80 percent of the room to raise their hand. My sense is that the other 20 percent are probably sitting next to their boss, staring straight ahead with their hands glued to the table. With that anecdotal evidence at play, it's fair to say that for those of us who've led for any length of time have been guilty of missing the mark on carefully considering the needs of others from time to time.

So let's get back to Cokegate 2015.

Imagine being one of those engineers. You've just spent a long day traveling across the plains of Iowa to a rural site. You stayed late into the night fixing a complicated system so the hospital could resume scanning patients in the morning. You fixed the system faster and with fewer parts than expected, yet you still know that staying for calibrations means not just dinner alone but that you're now going to miss your daughter's third soccer game in a row. As you scan the menu and decide whether to choose the salmon or the ribeye, you remember that the company isn't willing to buy you a beer, or even a root beer, to wash it down. I have to imagine that walking by the soda fountain and beer tap felt like a slap in the face, meal after meal, for that month or two when the decision was in place.

As I think back on the situation, I can't help but wonder what would've happened if the leader had brought the team *together* to *thoughtfully* share the concern and worked with the engineers to find ways to reduce costs. Instead, a well-intentioned but misguided policy was handed down with a bigger message to the team: *Your work today isn't worth a drink at dinner.*

Because this decision felt like par for the course for the way the engineering department was being treated in this season, no one spoke up and challenged it. Rather, I imagine there was a mix of eye rolls and people bringing just a little less heart to their work in response to feeling dishonored. The real kicker is that the cost of our engineering team believing that the leadership didn't appreciate their effort or care about the impact this decision had on them was so much higher than the cost of a couple of cases of Dr. Pepper or Michelob Light. Regardless of whether people try to go around the policy or leave the company over it, the impact of not carefully considering the impact of our decisions on people is deep, wide, and lasting.

Looking back, I'm not 100 percent sure how this decision was made or if it was ever even formally rolled out. But in many ways, when it comes to culture, perception is reality. Fortunately, it was eliminated with an apology almost as quickly as it had been handed down.

AMP It Up!

I love how clearly Dan Pink's *Drive* articulates three key characteristics that help to create a workplace culture that carefully considers the needs of others:

Autonomy: the desire to direct our own lives.

Mastery: the urge to make progress and improve in something that matters.

Purpose: the yearning to do what we do in service of something larger than ourselves.[6]

Beyond being properly compensated, people thrive when they have some level of freedom (autonomy), opportunities for growth (mastery), and the chance to be part of something meaningful (purpose). Beyond these general needs, each person on our team carries their own specific dreams, desires, and goals. As leaders, we'll never know everything about everyone, but it's amazing to watch leaders whose superpower is to listen to, be attentive to, and see people in remarkable ways. For some of the people we lead, it might be the hope of being a director someday; for others, they hope to earn and save enough to buy a house or fly to Tampa for their parents' fiftieth wedding anniversary.

A Moving Run

Though there are endless opportunities and thousands of examples, I'll share a couple of stories that come to mind when I think about putting skin on the bones

---

[6] Daniel H. Pink, *Drive: The Surprising Truth About What Motivates Us* (New York: Riverhead, 2009).

and what it looks like to bring thoughtful leadership to life.

Most days, a dozen or so team members gather at Planet Fitness to work out during the lunch hour. It just so happened to be a beautiful "Pure Michigan" day, so a couple of us decided to go for a run outside instead. Ever the 9:45-minute mile guy, I ended up side by side with one of our project managers for most of the run. As the miles ticked by, I asked him about his dreams for the future. Sometimes the question sounds like, "What do you want to be true in three years that isn't true today?" or in tongue-in-cheek fashion, "What do you want to do when you grow up?" Without skipping a beat, he shared that he hoped to grow in his role at Block Imaging and, in time, live closer to his family in the Northeast.

In the weeks that followed, I couldn't shake the certainty in his voice about wanting to live and raise children near his family. At the time, we were quite a bit smaller and more centralized at headquarters than we are today, so a remote role just wasn't in the cards. Despite not being able to make the first part of his dream come true, I felt a strong pull to help him chase his dream of being near family above what we could gain from him continuing in his role with us.

I scheduled a time with him and his leader to ask if he'd like our help and support in pursuing his dream to move out East. While he was initially a little nervous about changing locations and jobs simultaneously, he came back a week later with an air of excitement. We agreed for him to continue in his role while he pursued job opportunities, and within ninety days, he'd found a great fit, transitioned his responsibilities, and made it to the Northeast with his family just in time for Christmas.

Most of the time, someone's aspirations won't lead to us helping them leave the organization, but this is an example of unearthing what matters to people and partnering with them in accomplishing their hopes, dreams, and goals. *People matter* at work and in life!

Putting Theory into Practice

In March of 2020, nine years into leading the team at Block Imaging, my wife and I were on vacation in Mexico with some of our best friends. Over the course of the week, a virus that started on the other side of the world quickly made its way to us. One by one, events like NBA games, the Masters, and the entire NCAA Tournament were being canceled. I still remember when I realized our kids were being sent home from school and likely wouldn't return for the rest of the year! It became clear that COVID-19 would impact life and business for weeks, if not months. Little did we know it would reshape our lives for years to come.

As we flew home, I mentally prepared to communicate our response to the team. When I returned to the office, uncertainty hung thick in the air. Even amid so much unknown, with years of leading with the three T's under our belt, I felt more ready to tackle this season than I would have during my transition years before.

Different kinds of fear were circulating throughout the company, and the political atmosphere wasn't helping. In that moment, I was grateful for the culture of care we had cultivated over the years, because it paid dividends when we needed it most. As the virus spread and the news became more dire, I reflected on what *thoughtful* decisions would look like in this situation. While we couldn't control the pandemic or guarantee that no one would get sick, we could respond to people's concerns about their livelihoods. The most *thoughtful* decision we could communicate, backed by actions, was our intention to do everything possible to keep every team member employed from start to finish. That is exactly what we shared with the team and exactly what we set out to accomplish through the entirety of the pandemic. A little bit later in the book, I'll share more about the impact and outcome of sharing this goal at the outset.

Endless Opportunities

The options and opportunities really are boundless when we choose to lead through carefully considering the needs of others. For every person who has a compensation aspiration, another has a hope of leading others someday. And for every person who's looking for a promotion, another team member is looking for technical training, a hybrid work arrangement, or their retirement date in October. On the personal front, a team member who mentions that their daughter's third birthday is on Tuesday or that their mom is having an MRI to rule out a health issue or maybe that they're hoping to adopt a child someday are all opportunities to come alongside and support in a myriad of ways.

It's only Wednesday as I write this paragraph, but this week has already presented a wide range of life events happening in our team. One leader's brother was diagnosed with cancer, a sales rep's wife was in a car accident, a project manager is getting a CT scan, and another team member's son is playing in the soccer regional finals game tonight. Oh yeah, and earlier today I saw a cubicle decorated for an accounting team member's birthday and just received a reminder that it's the fourteenth work anniversary of one of our engineers. And as I was giving a customer tour after lunch, one of our leaders told me that two of our mechanical engineers are still out on the road after getting diverted to pick up a mammography system in Illinois. (Thank goodness they can enjoy a Coke or a Blue Moon tonight at dinner.) That may seem like a lot, and the reality is that it's but a fraction of what's going on across our organization!

Now, before you start thinking, "That's too much! How could I possibly manage all of that?" Remember it's not our job to do it all. While sometimes it might look like offering emotional or relational support and other times it might involve doing something more, it all starts with creating a culture where leaders care and are aware of what's important to those we lead. For bosses who live in the Me-Cycle, people are a burden, and their personal lives are a hindrance to what can be accomplished at work. I won't sugarcoat this one: If this is your mindset, you don't stand a chance of creating a culture where people thrive and bring their best. Because guess what . . . when bosses lead through the lens of the Me-Cycle, employees don't just know it—they feel it, and over time you'll be left with average team members who reciprocate with a lack of care for their work, their boss, and your organization.

"Hmm, that's interesting, Josh. Why did you say that I'll be left with the average ones?"

Great question. That's because over time, the best team members will depart for a We-Cycle culture where they can trust and be trusted, develop and be developed, and go home feeling appreciation for their leader, proud of their work, and connected to the mission.

If you've made it this far, I believe you're the kind of person who wants to create a We-Cycle culture. You're someone who cares for your team, but maybe you aren't quite sure how to walk it out yet. The first step is to shift our view from seeing and meeting the needs of people as a job or a burden to seeing it as an opportunity and a privilege. After all, when we care about what's important to the people we lead, some really amazing things start to happen.

Again, you can't and won't meet the needs of everyone every single time. That's impossible. But sometimes it looks like a one-minute text, and other times it's a quick, *thoughtful* check-in on Teams or in person that can make a world of difference. Maybe it's a note, or a gift card, or even sending pizza and breadsticks to the families of the mechanical team that's unexpectedly on the road tonight. Hold on a second while I send a quick message to a team member whose elderly dad hit his head while ice skating earlier this week . . .

You see where I'm going with this? Sometimes it's the littlest moments that make the biggest impact. I love the idea that the word *momentous* is rooted in the word *moment*. Lots of little brief points in time can stack up and change a culture and people's lives! The great news for us as leaders is that whatever we choose to model will become contagious and scale throughout the organization. When we make space for seeing and meeting the needs of others, it invites and sets a precedent for the entire team to follow.

Whether you're the CEO, lead a department, or are a brand-new hire, it starts with *you*. A few months ago, Emily Jones saw something that caught her eye on a team member's social media account. She instantly recognized a need behind the post, walked into my office, and said, "Could I please have some money to care for a team member?" After working side by side and watching Emily's superpower for seeing people unfold over the years, I've learned not to ask too many questions. The next day, I brought in $200 and handed her the cash.

Later, I learned she wrote a note from the entire Block Imaging team, put the cash in an envelope, and dropped it off on the person's desk. The next morning, with tears in his eyes, the team member walked over to Emily's desk to thank her for the way she saw him and went out of her way to help. Talk about an A+ example of taking careful consideration of the needs of others.

Be True to Your Context

I know what some of you might be thinking: "But Josh, my team is too small" or "I don't have the authority or resources for that." Insert your excuse of choice. While comparing and disregarding some of these stories might be tempting, this feels like a great time to again remind and implore you to **draft instead of compare.** These stories emerged from our context; the opportunities in yours may look really different.

Looking back on practicing deep care for all these years, it's important to note that many of the impactful moments cost nothing—like when two team members compiled a list of daycares, doctors, and dentists when Trevor moved his family from Denver. Total cost: $0. But the care he felt in the midst of relocating his young family across the country was significant. Creating meaningful moments for and with people is the investment of a lifetime. It really is impossible to overestimate the value of carefully considering the needs of those we work alongside, and it's what sets the Block Imaging culture apart.

Don't Do It Alone

When our new CFO, Rodrigo, relocated from Brazil in 2023, our team rallied around him in a way I just found out about recently. Here's what he shared about his first couple of months in the States:

> The first week I was here alone without my family, someone from my team brought food for a whole week. And I thought, "Oh, that is very nice. Thank you for the food." The next week, another person did, and I thought, "Okay, I like this." But then the third week and fourth week, we had three or four people bringing food. They said, "We know you are here by yourself, and you don't know a lot about the area. We want to help make this transition more gentle." And that was just the beginning. They don't bring me food anymore (which is a bummer), but the thoughtfulness has continued in so many ways.

In this case, it wasn't only one person who showed up for Rodrigo; it was his whole team. I've found over the years, as I'm confident you'll find as well, that when we as leaders see the needs of people, we will empower an army to see the needs of those around them too. A healthy culture ensures that the values that matter will express themselves far beyond your reach.

There was a time when I knew not only every team member's name but also the names of their significant other and children. Before the month began, I'd sit down and handwrite dozens of birthday and work-anniversary cards. But even then—and especially now with over four hundred team members—it's impossible for me to personally care for each person with any level of consistency. That's okay, because **caring for others is a team sport**, and it happens collectively just as much as it happens individually. When you show you care as a leader, people in your organization will be empowered to show others that they care too. We can't meet every single need, but I love Andy Stanley's mantra about guiding the way to leading people *thoughtfully*: **"Do for one what you wish you could do for everyone."**

It Starts with a Question

If you want to build a more *thoughtful* culture but don't know where to begin, start by asking questions. The questions will vary based on your role and relationship, but they all serve the same purpose: understanding what matters most to people.

"What's on your mind?" is a great question from the book *The Coaching Habit*.[7] This sort of open-ended question asked by someone who cares opens the window to a broad swathe of answers. Or here are a few others to try out:

"How's your family?" An upgrade is "How's Truett (or Amelia or Wyatt or Matteo)?"

"What's going well in your role, and what's most frustrating?"

"What do you hope to be true of you or your role in two years?"

"What's one thing you'd change about your role or department if you were in charge?"

Try it and see what happens. When someone shares that their son is playing T-ball or that they're overwhelmed, hoping to be a leader someday, or struggling with managing their team, it's a chance to respond—through words or actions—and in doing so, to build a more *thoughtful* culture. I can't emphasize enough the value in knowing what our people care about, even when we can't immediately meet every need, dream, or desire.

A little extra care from those with influence over budgets and compensation can go a long way. Setting aside a small portion of the budget to go above and

---

[7] Michael Bungay Stanier, *The Coaching Habit: Say Less, Ask More, and Change the Way You Lead Forever* (Herndon, Virginia: Page Two, 2016).

beyond to meet specific needs or to support people in meaningful ways can take us way further than a small cost-of-living increase. I love how Chip and Dan Heath talk about the impact of "breaking the script" in their book *The Power of Moments*:

"Our lives are measured in moments, and defining moments are the ones that endure in our memories." One of my favorite quotes from the book reminds us to "beware of the soul-sucking force of reasonableness" when it comes to seeing and creating moments for the people we lead.[8]

I love that. Giving someone a gift card to Pizza Hut is special but reasonable. It's an entirely different ball game to send a family a pizza party when you find out their child had their braces removed, just got released from the hospital, or got their black belt in karate. Give it a shot, and I think you'll find some of the best unexpected moments for you, your team, and your organization.

Finances and Workspaces

Regardless of your place on the org chart, we have the privilege of growing our awareness of what's important to people—individually and collectively. After leading

---

[8] Chip Heath and Dan Heath, *The Power of Moments: Why Certain Experiences Have Extraordinary Impact* (New York: Simon and Schuster, 2017).

for more than a decade, I began to notice two areas that require special attention and sensitivity within our teams.

The first is *anything related to finances*, whether it be compensation or other benefits. From raises to work-boot stipends, mileage reimbursements, dental coverage, and 401(k) matches, these decisions affect people's livelihoods and also impact security and worth. It's extra important to be so incredibly *thoughtful* in how we approach, implement, and articulate compensation decisions.

Just last week, I was in a conversation with one of our HR business partners. A few members of the team had shared some concerns about our approach to "stand-by" or on-call compensation. Given the specifics of the situation, the governmental regulations in one particular state were pretty difficult to interpret. While arguing over rules and policy is common in a Me-Cycle world, in looking through the lens of carefully considering the needs of others, I asked our HR partner a couple of questions to help chart a course forward *together*.

"Do we know how many after-hours calls a team member receives on a given day or week?"

"No," they said. "We're not really sure."

"Okay. Having a sense of the volume of calls would be really helpful. Do we know whether those calls are usually during the day or in the middle of the night? Are they typically a short disruption, or do they commonly interrupt the team member for more than a few minutes?"

Not really sure of the call frequency, duration, or time of day, another team member jumped in and elaborated that when a call is received, full pay or even overtime rates are given during the call.

"Okay, that's great," I said. "But if you were interrupted three times during dinner and took four minutes each time to take the call and create a ticket, would twelve minutes of pay be appropriate given the circumstances?"

Probably not.

At the end of the day, it's impossible to carefully consider the needs of others if we aren't acutely aware of what's going on in their world. If the team takes one three-minute call... in the evening... every seven days, most would agree that the current structure is pretty reasonable. However, if they're taking a large volume of short calls, half of which are in the middle of the night, it probably makes sense to approach our compensation model differently.

Lastly, while compensation is often a high-stakes topic, my sense is that a situation like this is as much an issue of understanding as it is about the money. Without understanding, the team isn't sure that we're aware of what's going on; and if we aren't up to speed, we certainly can't acknowledge or appreciate their efforts. On the other hand, when we take the time to ask questions, listen, and understand, we not only express our care through attention but we become better equipped to build a more *thoughtful* approach for the team.

The second sensitive area relates to *workspaces*. Whether it's the layout, lighting, temperature, noise level, proximity to coworkers in an office or cubicle, or the condition of a work truck, people tend to care deeply about their work environments. And it makes sense—team members spend more time in their workspaces than almost anywhere except their beds. While it may not always be possible to give everyone exactly what they want, it's important to recognize how much these details affect people's lives. Decisions around office layouts, cubicle configurations, furniture, and meeting rooms can be easy to overlook if we don't pay attention to how much they impact people's lives.

As leaders, it can be especially easy to dismiss or diminish decisions that don't seem like a big deal to us. Sometimes, if we're not mindful, we tend to overlook things that we take for granted. (Excuse me while I shut my door to send an email telling a team member it shouldn't matter that their workspace isn't private.) Ahem. Okay, I'm back.

When we start imposing what we think should matter on those we lead, we've missed the mark. If office temperature and dental plans are important to our people, they ought to be important to us. In these moments, we can either focus on ourselves or focus on the needs of others. While you likely have a lot on your plate, there's great value in slowing down to *thoughtfully* consider how each decision, especially in the realm of compensation and workspaces, impacts the work and fulfillment of the people we lead.

Measuring the Impact

While I might still be a young leader with lots of new responsibilities, making decisions *together* has a way of multiplying wisdom and serves as a gateway to becoming a thoughtful leader. It didn't take long for the team to sense and appreciate that diligence and precision. The focus on *thoughtful* decision-making had a profound impact in two distinct ways.

First, each decision—large or small—began to set a precedent for future decisions across the organization. Over time, the expectation grew that this *thoughtful* approach would trickle through to the entire team. My careful consideration for the needs of others would in time become *our careful consideration for the needs of people*.

Second, *thoughtful* decision-making stifled the far-too-common post-decision watercooler conversations. So much energy is wasted and traction lost when people second-guess decisions behind the scenes and after the fact. This doesn't just waste time; it undermines credibility and crushes morale. By being *thoughtful*, we helped minimize skepticism and suspicion, redirecting the team's energy away from idle complaints and toward positive contributions.

Just like living out the *together* principle, in the world of organizational decision-making and culture-shaping, being *thoughtful* is the ounce of prevention that's worth a pound of cure.

Keep on Truckin'

Here's another example of how working *together* to make *thoughtful* decisions looks in practice. A couple of years back, we discussed adding a new transport vehicle to our service fleet. Our vehicles cover a wide range of situations, and it can be tricky to determine the perfect one to accommodate everything from moving a CT scanner across the country to picking up multiple systems along the way. Some vehicles are more comfortable, others more capable, so there were differing opinions on what we should purchase and why.

Our leader of technical excellence heard that some team members thought we needed a van, while others leaned toward a pickup or box truck. In response, he asked if a team lead from another department would gather input from several technical team members to help decide exactly what we should purchase. It took a month or two, but the team eventually homed in on the perfect truck with the right capacity, power, and features to safely transport equipment nationwide. Because the team had been involved from the beginning, excitement started building as the truck's arrival approached.

And let's not miss a key piece here. There's a *huge* difference between (a) a truck simply showing up and hearing after the fact whether people thought it was a great or crappy decision and (b) the team anticipating its arrival while jokingly debating who would get to drive it first. That really happened, and the winner of rock, paper, scissors drove the truck into the headquarters parking lot with the horn ripping and people cheering. Over the next hour, the team members who would ride in this truck for endless hours to come welcomed the rest of the team out to take a tour as they shared with pride how the new gadgetry would impact their everyday work.

In the grand scheme of everything that's happening at Block Imaging, this is just one of many decisions that are made on a daily basis. But each decision brings with it not only responsibility but opportunity as well. Remember what I said about workspaces? While purchasing the truck could have just as easily been viewed as a run-of-the-mill business decision, in carefully considering the needs of the men and women who would be riding in it for thousands and thousands of hours and miles, it led to a moment of pride and a deep sense of ownership for the new vehicle.

Fast-forward to our Christmas party six months later when a woman approached me with tears in her eyes, asking to speak to her husband's leader.

Months earlier, her husband had accidentally driven that brand-spanking-new box truck into a place where . . . let's just say the truck was taller than the overhang. As the engineer drove back to headquarters late on a Friday night, he was discouraged and clearly embarrassed by the mistake. Instead of letting him carry the weight of that error alone into the weekend, his leader met him at the facility. Rather than chastising or poking fun at him, he welcomed the team member back and encouraged him to let it go and enjoy the weekend. This small but *thoughtful* act made a big difference not just to this engineer but to his wife, who had one mission in mind when she showed up at that Christmas party: to find and personally thank her husband's leader for his response to the truck accident. The way we handle situations great and small matters and undoubtedly shapes the culture of our organization and our people's lives beyond the office!

Capacity Building

Before diving into the third T, I want to highlight that **culture building is capacity building.** While anything worth doing is usually hard at first, in the chapters to come we'll dig into how leaning into the three T's actually serves to reduce the weight and increase capacity for leaders. So let's keep moving forward, because right after digging into the third T, we're going to take a look at how people feel and respond to being led with courage, conviction, and care.

Here's where we are on the We-Cycle:

Level Up

If you haven't been intentional in being a *thoughtful* leader but want to start, here's a simple first step: Share what you're learning with your team. Be vulnerable. Tell them you want to be a leader who considers the impact of your decisions on them more *thoughtfully*.

Acknowledge a time when you missed the mark, and share your commitment to being more deliberate in the season ahead. If you're genuine, your team will appreciate the sentiment and will be watching carefully to see how you grow in the way you carefully consider the needs of others going forward.

Keeping It Real

Becky
Marketing Specialist | 7 years at Block

When I joined Block Imaging in 2018, my children were just two and five years old. I was commuting over forty-five minutes each way, trying to navigate a new job while juggling motherhood. A few months in, I got that dreaded call from my childcare provider: "One of your children is sick." At my previous job, moments like that came with guilt and judgment. I was afraid of letting people down. But when I told my leader what was going on, they simply said, "GO. That's where you're needed most." The very next day, they opened our conversation by asking how my child was doing. I knew in that moment: I was cared for as a person and as a mom.

At Block, I've found a place where growth is encouraged and supported. Resources for development, conflict resolution, and healthy dialogue aren't just available—they're part of how we work. I'm not just an employee: I'm an active participant in shaping my career, my team's culture, and the company's future.

One moment I'll never forget was when I was exploring a new professional opportunity on another team. When I shared this with my leader, I expected hesitation. Instead, he said, "Let's talk through how your strengths, goals, and ideas align with this potential role so I can advocate for you." That kind of support, even when it could lead to a ton of extra work hiring and training my successor, showed me what leadership that truly puts people first looks like.

Celebration is woven into our culture—balloons for birthdays, shout-outs during all-team meetings, and Post-it notes left on keyboards with simple messages like "I couldn't have done it without you." These moments may seem small, but they leave a lasting impact.

I am the leader, wife, and mother I am today in part because of my time at Block. I've learned to welcome challenge, embrace feedback, and seek bold conversations because here, growth isn't something to fear. It's something to pursue.

At Block, your dreams, your voice, your joy, and even your pain are safe. You can speak up, offer new ideas, and advocate for yourself because here, *people matter* isn't just a phrase. It's how we live.

CHAPTER 6

Open the Window to *Transparency*

As we sought to create a place where people loved to work, respected their leaders, appreciated their organization, felt connected to the mission, and went home more equipped than when they arrived, a third T, *transparency*, rose to the surface alongside *together* and *thoughtful*. Looking back, I'm so grateful for the ways these principles rose up organically and flowed out so authentically. Also, the fact that all three words started with the letter *T* was convenient, if not serendipitous!

Defining *Transparency*

Just like the word *thoughtful*, after years of practicing *transparency*, I decided to look up its formal definition.

Also like *thoughtful*, the definition isn't all that provocative at first glance. But similar to any good 2:00 a.m. infomercial selling duct tape that can seal a baseball-sized hole in a canoe, "But wait, there's more!" In the context of leadership and company culture, *transparency* is best boiled down to three powerful qualities:

- free from pretense or deceit
- readily understood
- open, not secretive

The only thing better than a leader who works *together* to make *thoughtful* decisions is putting a cherry on top by being open, honest, and easy to understand!

The Minimalist Approach: A Dangerous Path

Lots of leaders and organizations operate with a "less is more" mindset when it comes to sharing information. Positional or Me-Cycle leadership often begins by asking, "What do people absolutely have to know to show up and do their jobs?"

For some, hoarding information is a form of job security. Others think the people they lead don't care, can't understand, or don't deserve to know what's going on. Regardless of the reasoning, it's pretty wild to hear that Gallup's 2023 poll revealed that less than 30 percent of US workers strongly agree that their immediate supervisor keeps them informed about what's happening in the organization. A similar percentage somewhat agree that they're well informed. That leaves over 40 percent of people who place themselves on the "uninformed" end of the spectrum—a diminishing, disorienting, and frustrating experience.

When bosses withhold information, it's only natural for a team to feel unimportant and for their level of engagement and sense of ownership to decline. And when those two things start to happen, the weight of leadership grows, weariness sets in, and resentment starts to build from both sides. Those "in charge" feel a lack of support from the team, while employees feel like cogs in a machine. This vicious Me-Cycle is far too common and quite the opposite of what we're after in creating a healthy and successful team culture.

A Different Approach: Maximizing *Transparency*

When it comes to leading with *transparency*, we've found tremendous benefit in testing the opposite approach to Me-Cycle subterfuge. From strategy and financial performance to business opportunities and challenges, we've opted for maximum *transparency*. Instead of sharing the bare minimum, we've started from a place of sharing as much information as we possibly can without compromising our team's privacy or the company's well-being.

In taking *transparency* for a test drive (and buying it over and over again), the litmus test for what remains confidential hasn't changed much since we began in 2011: **Does keeping this information private protect the individual, the team, or the company?**

In response to that question, here are the areas we've been intentional about protecting:

Personal Information: Compensation, individual performance, health, or family issues.
Owner's Box Information: Equity, shareholder distributions, and legal agreements.
Legally Restricted Information: Any situation where legal obligations prevent us from sharing details.

Despite some initial skepticism, this max-*transparency* approach has served us well through the course of enduring growth.

Three Questions to Drive *Transparency*

After practicing maximum *transparency* for quite a few years, three key questions emerged in providing a guide of sorts to leading with *transparency*.

OPEN THE WINDOW TO *TRANSPARENCY*

People wanna know → What's going on?

This question focuses on the big picture. From direction to strategy, challenges, opportunities, and priorities, the more we as leaders share, the more trust and alignment we build. When we're *transparent* about financial performance, targets, upcoming decisions, or even roadblocks, we invite people to lean in and help solve problems and seize opportunities.

Sometimes the small topics have an outsized impact on people. For example, one fall, we noticed that we were quickly outgrowing the number of parking spaces in the lots at our Michigan headquarters. While this might seem like a fairly innocuous matter, it took ninety seconds to proactively provide an update at our October all-team meeting:

"Hey team, we see that the number of cars is growing quickly, and there are times when we don't have enough parking spaces at HQ. Since it's winter and we won't be able to expand the lot until the spring, we appreciate your creativity in navigating our parking constraints over the winter months."

While it's a small act of *transparency*, it signaled to everyone that we were (a) aware of the issue and (b) working *together* on a *thoughtful* solution. No one expects us to break ground on an asphalt parking lot in the heart of a Michigan winter. But it's natural for people to expect to have a parking space when they show up to work, so we honor that missed expectation when we acknowledge that we see and have a *thoughtful* plan to address the growing concern.

Team Meetings and Fail Tales

For the last twelve years, we've held a company-wide meeting on the third Thursday of every month. These meetings now have more than two hundred attending in person and two hundred joining virtually from all over the world. We get off and running by reminding people that we are a question-asking culture. Each person in the room has a card and pen on their chair to participate in the Q&A session, and members joining online can participate via the online chat.

From there, we celebrate recent birthdays and work anniversaries before we announce open positions, share key business updates, have a customer spotlight, and share a monthly financial update that shows our actual results compared to the annual target. Sometimes we leave a couple of minutes for contests like our two-minute NCAA Tournament bracket game in March or Christmas trivia in December. Before ending with an open Q&A, we spend a few minutes on what we call "kudos" and "fail tales." Kudos is our time for people to share recent stories about team members who've gone above and beyond, and a fail tale is when someone openly shares a mistake they've made in the last month.

Celebrating one another and learning from mistakes are central to who we are. As organizations expand, there's a growing tendency to hide mistakes for fear of consequences. The reality is that mistakes are part of business and life, and encouraging people to take responsibility with *transparency* and to get better *together* reinforces trust. Oftentimes, we'll see a kudo and fail tale merge when someone shares about how another team member helped to rescue them during or after a mistake was made.

Over the course of more than 150 all-team meetings, we've fielded more than a thousand questions that range from facility upgrades to benefits; parts harvesting to empowering women in leadership; and what we're most proud of, concerned about, or are asking of the team.

Beyond honoring our commitment to *transparency*, the Q&A sessions have brought about several other benefits:

> **Awareness:** The questions people ask help to grow our leaders' awareness of what's on the team's mind. We learn more about what they are focused on, interested in, and concerned or excited about. Q&A sessions are incredibly potent for understanding what the team is thinking about.

Growth: Question-asking fosters a culture of learning, curiosity, and growth! Good questions lead to the team gaining more context, which equips them to ask better questions. As the wheel of questions and context turns, we become stronger as a team.

Unity: Answering questions breaks down the walls between leaders and teams. The team can ask whatever they're curious about, and we'll do our best to provide insight and clarity. The ivory tower syndrome is real, and Q&A is an effective tool to tear it down by giving both the leaders and the team time to be real with one another.

This rhythm reinforces the message that we don't have a secret veil with a bunch of information behind it that's too complex for them to understand. We want our team to know what's going on, because we believe they play an integral role in shaping who we're becoming and where we're going as a company.

These meetings are so crucial that we pause all operations for an hour every month as we come *together* to recognize where we're at, equip our people with key information, and lean into where we're going as a team. It's a blast to see the boost that comes from everyone coming *together*, sharing stories, laughing out loud, celebrating one another, and ultimately busting down the walls that are built when people feel left in the dark.

People wanna know → <u>What are you thinking?</u>

This question dives a little deeper. Beyond knowing what's going on, our team members want to know what the leader is thinking, excited, concerned, or learning about. When we share what we're chewing on, even when ideas aren't fully formed, we empower the team to think beyond their immediate tasks and consider the problems that are holding the team back. When we share what books we're reading or podcasts we're listening to, we invite the team around us into engaging, developmental content. Lastly, when we share that we spent an afternoon whiteboarding about the year ahead, we highlight the value of creating a vision for the future.

Transparency in the Unknown

Transparency becomes even more critical in times of uncertainty. Take the onset of the COVID-19 pandemic, when no one knew what to expect. Having built a culture of *transparency* for years, we chose to share information as openly and as often as we could, even though the situation was constantly shifting and people carried vastly different opinions on what was really taking place. Half of the people on our team were afraid for their lives; the other half were afraid for their jobs. As the news and the virus spread around the world, it was one thing to make a *thoughtful* decision and something entirely different to communicate it openly with the team.

Given that our organization supports radiology departments on the front lines of healthcare, some of our team members were delivering equipment to hospitals, and we sent a large portion of our team home to work remotely for a season. As I mentioned earlier, during a town hall in March of 2020, we shared this message: "As we move through this pandemic, our number one goal is to do everything we can to make sure everyone on this team is paid from start to finish."

In communicating our goal, we were sharing—in no uncertain terms—*you matter and your families matter.* While we couldn't guarantee how long the pandemic would last or that we'd be successful as a company, we could be *transparent* in sharing what we as leaders were after. And that was just the beginning. From task forces to remote work to distancing, contact tracing, and ultimately articulating our approach to the vaccine, *thoughtful* and *transparent* were a powerful one-two punch in this unique season.

Financial *Transparency*: Data on Display

One of the boldest moves we've made in the pursuit of *transparency* was the decision to share our financial results with the entire team. Several business leaders discouraged us, saying it was too risky and that once people knew the organization's profitability, they might grow resentful or ask for raises more frequently.

Well, we did it anyway, and we haven't looked back since. In our high-trust hearts, we believed not only that our team could handle the information but that their awareness and engagement would make us stronger. To this day, we share monthly updates with the entire team on revenue, gross margin, and net income in relation to the previous year and current targets. We have a company-wide bonus plan based on global profitability, so the team tangibly benefits when we win *together*. We sometimes celebrate being ahead of the target and hitting the goal. Other times (like last week) we share that we're behind after the first quarter and offer some key priorities that will help us close the gap.

People Moving

Another area where we seek to lead with transparency is how we approach people entering, moving throughout, and exiting the organization. One of the things we've discussed as leaders is how we use *chemistry, competency,* and *character* as a framework for guiding these decisions.

1. *Chemistry*: Do you work well with your leader and others on your team? If the answer is yes, great. If there's a struggle in this regard, we'll do

everything we can to see if there's a better fit in the organization.
2. *Competency*: Are you effective in your role? Similar to chemistry, if there's a gap in this space, we will do everything we can to see if there's a better role in the organization to match up with a team member's capabilities or offer growth opportunities when appropriate.
3. *Character*: While we love to believe in people and extend second chances often, we've been really clear that this is the only fast track *out of* our organization. I jokingly say that "your momma taught you what you know about character, and if she didn't do a good job, we probably won't either."

While we've seen our fair share of complex situations, having a framework for team member transitions and sharing that we tend to be more patient and creative when it comes to *chemistry* and *competency* than we are with matters of character is incredibly honoring to the team. And it helps to frame everyone's expectations for thriving within their team.

People wanna know → What are you thinking about me?

While leaning into *transparency* around questions 1 (What's going on?) and 2 (What are you thinking?) is powerful, this one (What are you thinking *about me?*) is a total game changer. In my experience, this is where most leaders lack the courage and tools necessary to lead with care and clarity. In turn, this is where they face the greatest deficit and where the biggest opportunity lies.

The reality is, *most* team members wish they knew *more* about what their leader was *really* thinking about their performance. *Thoughtful* feedback strengthens trust and fuels performance, and yet, through the guise of being kind or keeping the peace, so many leaders shy away from offering clear and consistent feedback. Remember that statistic about engagement I shared with you? Only one-third of US employees were engaged in a recent Gallup survey. But check this out. Just one year later, the Gallup survey showed that 80 percent of people who received meaningful feedback in the past week were fully engaged at work. Whoa! The tie between feedback and engagement is pretty extraordinary.

One of my favorite Brené Brown quotes, **"clear is kind,"** absolutely nails it when it comes to feedback. The 2011 book *Crucial Conversations* puts it another way when it speaks to the value of being 100 percent honest and 100 percent respectful.[9] Many people believe they

---

[9] Kerry Patterson, Joseph Grenny, Ron McMillan, and Al Switzler, *Crucial Conversations: Tools for Talking When Stakes Are High* (New York: McGraw-Hill, 2002).

are being kind by not sharing feedback, but the reality is that we are harming ourselves, the other person, and our organizations by not building the muscles of offering and receiving feedback.

Feedback Matters

When it comes to feedback loops and the power of *transparency*, I'll never forget this feedback "mic drop" moment with one of our VPs, Amy Somerville. I had dropped by a Chick-fil-A to grab lunch before having our 1:1 over the phone while driving back from Fort Wayne, Indiana. I asked a few questions so Amy would do most of the talking while I mowed down waffle fries and chicken fingers before they had a chance to reach room temperature. In the midst of wiping Polynesian sauce from my beard, Amy casually shared a story about a recent performance assessment she had conducted. At the end of the review, she told the team member, **"That is all the feedback I have for you. I'm holding nothing back."**

In one simple sentence, Amy embodied *transparency* at its finest. In so many leadership relationships, team members are left to wonder, "But what does the boss *really* think of me?" After all, it's one thing to satisfy HR by checking the box and stuffing the file with a performance assessment document. But it's an entirely different story to honor the team member with *transparency* by taking the time to share meaningful feedback. Topics like progress, growth opportunities, and the attitudes and behaviors you appreciate and want to invite them into strengthening are perfectly suited for performance assessments.

In response to an absence of feedback, people are forced to (a) not care, (b) assume you're not thinking much about them, or (c) speculate about the filing cabinets of feedback you've withheld from them. And the worst part? This lack of feedback leads team members to land on one end of the false assumption spectrum. On one side is an overly inflated view of themselves, through which they see no concerns or opportunities for growth. But more commonly, people tend to fall on the other side, where they fill the gaps with their own overwhelmingly negative and inaccurate feedback. In either case, people are left in the dark and robbed of growth and development opportunities. "That is all the feedback I have for you. I'm holding nothing back" has become a gold standard when it comes to offering feedback and leading with *transparency*.

Go First

For better or worse, if we want to build a feedback-driven culture, one of the best ways to foster it is to *go first*. The healthiest relationships are formed when feedback is a two-way street, and there's no better way to demonstrate humility and teachability than by asking for feedback from your team.

"What's one thing I can do to better equip you in this season?"

"What's one thing you'd do differently if you were in my shoes?"

"What's one thing I'm doing that helps the team and one thing I'm doing that hurts the team?"

But here's the deal: Showing your team you're serious about wanting their feedback takes time. Initially, most people will play it safe and test the waters by tossing us an easy one. When we thank them for their feedback and follow through with their suggestion, they start to realize that we genuinely care about their thoughts and that we're striving to grow as leaders. This creates an environment in which *transparent*, two-way feedback becomes the norm.

A Broken Record

As with most valuable things, *transparency* isn't always easy, but not being *transparent* is much more costly. In nearly every keynote session I lead, there's a point toward the end when I open up the floor for Q&A. After answering countless questions over the years, I began to notice a haunting pattern. While the questions often sounded unique because of their specific context, the answers had a consistent theme as it relates to *transparency*. Here's a typical exchange:

"So, Josh, I have this team member who is doing something that is negatively impacting the team. I feel like I've tried everything, but nothing has worked. What would you suggest?"

My response is generally along the lines of "Thanks for the question. Have you spoken with the person specifically about the concern and how their behavior is impacting the team?"

The answers tend to be pretty predictable: "Kinda, but it didn't change anything," "Well, I did file a report with HR a while back. They really should know better," or perhaps my favorite, "I sent the message through a team lead," or something along these lines.

While the responses differ slightly, they often carry an air of passivity and hopelessness. And the truth of the matter is that if we're unwilling to lead and address the issues head on, it is pretty hopeless. Whether it's an opportunity for growth or if a team member's attitudes or actions fall short of our expectations, it's both a privilege and responsibility as leaders to provide direct and honest feedback. It might feel uncomfortable at first, but it's essential. Brushing things under the rug isn't helpful in closing the gap between where someone is and where we expect them to be. Over time, this unspoken gap erodes trust, impacts performance, and breeds resentment—not just between the leader and that team member, but throughout the entire team.

Muscle Building: Reps Are Better Than Weight

When it comes to feedback, it's key to start early and offer it often. **Feedback serves to strengthen and draw those with a growth mindset because it's a gift to the hungry and humble.** In other words, our best people want more feedback. Yes, giving feedback can feel uncomfortable at first (especially if you're leading people who were once your peers), but discomfort is a small price to pay when it comes to inviting people into new growth opportunities. Just like anything we practice with intention, the more we do it, the easier it becomes.

One of the biggest pain points in the realm of building feedback muscles is simply not giving or receiving enough. Leaders often hold back, waiting for formal reviews or annual assessments. This approach tends to place too much pressure and stress on these few and far between moments. When feedback is infrequent, it tends to carry much more weight than is beneficial for trust and development. Instead, **the key is to keep feedback loops short and frequent.** Sharing feedback regularly becomes part of the leadership rhythm, allowing it to be received as a sign of care and belief rather than as critique or disappointment. Frequent feedback also moves the focus from dramatic shifts to small refinements. When feedback is offered *thoughtfully* and consistently, it's far more likely to be embraced as a tool for growth rather than as a weight to carry.

At the end of the day, if the person's growth is more important than our comfort, we should be willing to step into discomfort to help that person get better. Feedback is an act of courage and care. It shows that we value a person enough to invest in their development.

As always, there's a fine line between being constructively *transparent* and overly critical; **the goal is to equip, encourage, and empower, not to tear down or be impossible to please.** Hopefully, as you offer more feedback, your team will feel safe enough to give you feedback as well, creating a virtuous cycle of growth.

Again, Clear Is Kind

So, what happens when we've been clear, but there's no change? If you've been *transparent* and consistent, but the gap still isn't closing, it's likely time for a high-stakes conversation. Here's an example of a clear and, believe it or not, kind message:

"We're going to have a high-stakes conversation today. Over the past several months, I've shared my concerns about your (fill in the blank: follow-up with customers, ability to work well with others, negativity, sales performance, etc.). This is critical to your success and the team's success, and it's a baseline expectation for being part of this team. Out of care for you and the team, it's important to know that if we're unable to close the gap between where we are today and where we need to be over the next (x) months, it will be time to bring closure to your time as part of this team."

"Whoa, Josh. With how hard that was to read, I can't even imagine saying it."

At first glance, that might be really uncomfortable to read for some of us. There's no doubt that it's direct, but the question is whether it's more kind to (a) say something up front so that they have clarity around the concerns and consequences, (b) work around them endlessly, or (c) build up resentment and a case file, only to wake up one day to fire them because you finally reached the end of your rope.

While a high-stakes conversation may be momentarily uncomfortable, it's simply taking a situation that's been a little uncomfortable over a long period of time and making it a lot more uncomfortable for a short time. Furthermore, it's taking an issue that has likely impacted many people and focusing it on the only two people who can close the gap: the leader and the team member. This is our invitation as leaders.

Guardrails for *Transparency*

Before wrapping up our discussion on *transparency*, it's important that we install some guardrails. *Transparency* is powerful, but it can be misused if not applied with careful consideration for the needs of others. Here's what *transparency* is not:

- **It's not a "my way or the highway" power play.** *Transparency* should be about clarity, not control. The goal is to serve the team members by providing context and handholds for success through open and honest communication.
- **It's not an excuse to vent personal frustrations.** Being *transparent* doesn't mean complaining about your boss, coworkers, or family to others.
- **It's not about micromanaging.** *Transparency* isn't about nitpicking every detail. Focus on what truly matters for growth and success. If it's not moving the needle on performance or culture, it's probably not worth emphasizing.

Now that we've explored *transparency* in more depth, let's take a look at the We-Cycle with all three T's in play.

Level Up

Let's take a look at a couple of questions as they relate to leading with *transparency*:

- *What's going on?*
  What am I holding back from my team? What would the benefit be of sharing a little bit more here?

OPEN THE WINDOW TO TRANSPARENCY

- *What am I, as their leader, thinking about?*
  What could I share that would give people insight into what I'm thinking about, concerned about, or excited about?

- *As their leader, what am I thinking about them?*
  Is there something I've been holding back from sharing with a team member that I'd like to see them grow in? Why haven't I shared it yet?

Keeping It Real

Tyler

Regional Account Executive | 8 years at Block

People matter came alive for me from the very beginning. From the way the team celebrated my first day to the recognition of my hundred-day milestone, it was clear this wasn't just a phrase—it was a culture people truly lived. The early milestones gave me momentum, but one hard conversation in 2022 changed everything.

After four years on our service team, I was given the opportunity to step into a sales role and relocate my family to Orlando. It was an exciting move, but eighteen months in, it was clear things weren't going well. I hadn't delivered the results I was brought in for. My activity was low. My confidence was fading. And the gap between what I was capable of and what I was producing was only growing.

Given our long-standing relationship, Josh reached out and asked for a call. I knew it wouldn't be easy—and it wasn't. He didn't sugarcoat anything. He told me plainly: He was concerned about the results but even more concerned about my effort. Then he laid out three options:

1. Shift to a different role—though he couldn't recommend it based on where we were.
2. Part ways with Block and pursue a role at another company.
3. Go all in—recommit fully, raise the bar, and give it everything I had.

That conversation hit hard—but it didn't knock me down. It woke me up. For the first time in a long time, I felt truly *seen*. Not as a failure but as someone still worth fighting for. I chose Option 3.

Josh didn't just issue a challenge; he equipped me for the road back. He set expectations, added accountability, and offered me the structure I needed to push off the bottom and start swimming again. That conversation became the turning point in my career. It lit a fire I didn't know I had, and I haven't looked back since.

Three years later, I'm thriving in my role and now have the privilege of leading a new member of our sales team. That "last-ditch college try" became the first step in a journey toward greater discipline, deeper resilience, and lasting transformation. And the impact didn't stop at the office. It's made me a better husband. A better father. A better teammate. The very role I once thought I might lose has become part of a thriving, high-performing team I'm proud to help build.

If I had to sum up *People Matter at Work* in one word, it would be *serve*. It's about putting others first—whether that's a teammate, a customer, or your family. It means seeing people not just for who they are today but for who they can become. That's what Josh did for me. That moment redefined my story, and every day since, I've tried to lead others with the same courage and care.

PART III

The We-Cycle @ Work

While my hope to create a healthy culture started from the beginning, deep and lasting cultural change didn't happen overnight. As the months turned into years, we started to feel some progress by putting people first and embodying the three T's. At first, positive momentum looked like team members encouraging their friends to join the team. Before long, I began to hear people outside of our organization saying nice things, and our team was speaking with pride about who we were becoming. While anecdotal evidence was certainly refreshing, we began performing an engagement survey across the entire organization in 2016. With 97 percent team participation, of those surveyed:

97 percent said they've had opportunities to learn and grow in the past year.

96 percent said that the mission of the company makes them feel their job is important.

99 percent said their manager cares about them as a person.

47 percent said they have a best friend at work.

Those first results were off the charts in the realm of team engagement, and they would serve as gas in the tank to keep us going and growing! While it's the leader's privilege and responsibility to get the We-Cycle spinning by working *together* to make *thoughtful* decisions and to lead with *transparency*, it was a blast to see how people "We-Spond" (see what I did there) and in turn "We-Act" (there it is again) when leaders embody the three T's with care and consistency.

CHAPTER 7

The Three S's

While it doesn't happen overnight and everyone's response is a little different, when leaders put in the time, effort, heart, and intentionality of the three T's, it's natural for team members to feel *safe*, *seen*, and *successful* at work.

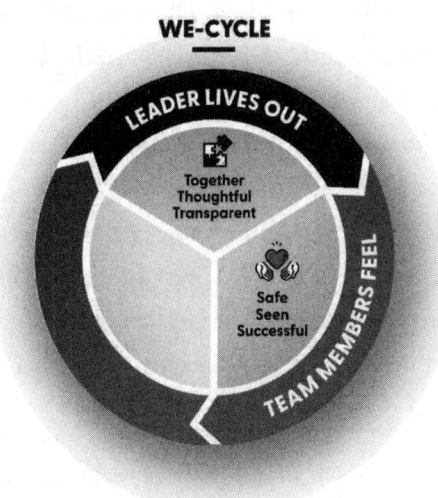

Safety's No Accident

While physical safety is incredibly important, fostering psychological safety is instrumental in creating a culture where people thrive and love to work. I love how Amy C. Edmondson speaks to this in her book *The Fearless Organization*.

> Psychological safety is broadly defined as a climate in which people are comfortable expressing and being themselves. More specifically, when people have psychological safety at work, they feel comfortable sharing concerns and mistakes without fear of embarrassment or retribution. They are confident they can speak up and won't be humiliated, ignored, or blamed. They know they can ask questions when they are unsure about something. They tend to trust and respect their colleagues. When a work environment has reasonably high psychological safety, good things happen: mistakes are reported quickly so that prompt corrective action can be taken; seamless coordination across groups or departments is enabled, and potentially game-changing ideas for innovation are shared. In short, psychological safety is a crucial source of value creation in organizations operating in a complex, changing environment.[10]

---

[10] Amy C. Edmondson, *The Fearless Organization: Creating Psychological Safety in the Workplace for Learning, Innovation, and Growth*

THE THREE S'S

Earlier in the book, I shared the parallel between culture and air quality. In healthy organizations, people feel *safe* to take risks, *safe* to speak up, *safe* to lean into high-stakes conversations, *safe* to acknowledge mistakes, *safe* to teach those around them, and *safe* to bring creativity to the way they serve customers. In other words, people can breathe! **In toxic cultures where fear abounds, people are far more likely to avoid conflict, withhold information, hide mistakes, and play it safe by holding back and operating within the status quo. There's no air.**

Let's take a moment to correlate safety with the three T's. When bosses don't unite others to strengthen decisions, don't carefully consider the needs of team members, and leave people in the dark, it's only natural for people to feel unsafe. In these scenarios, people don't have the confidence to speak up and as a result aren't able to bring their best. But when leaders work *together*, we protect people and the organization by making better decisions. When we make *thoughtful* decisions, we foster psychological safety by asking, "How will this decision impact the people on the other side?" **Lastly, when we lead with transparency, through equipping and empowering people, we increase their sense of security and they're free to be creative and take risks.**

(New York: Wiley, 2018).

See It to Believe It

I had the opportunity to speak at a conference last weekend and had the privilege of meeting psychiatrist Dr. Curt Thompson. During his session, Thompson shared that "we all are born into the world looking for someone looking for us." Put more simply, people want to be seen.

When it comes to seeing people, the difference between the Me-Cycle and the We-Cycle is enormous. In the Me-Cycle, everyone's looking into the proverbial mirror and in turn seeing *themselves*! From overlooked to replaceable, employees feel like a number or object. But when we lean and live into the We-Cycle—when we work *together* to make *thoughtful* decisions—we *see* people in some pretty extraordinary and uncommon ways.

When we lead with *transparency*, we're in essence saying, **"We see you, and we think your awareness and understanding of what's going on in the organization and what I'm thinking about you in particular is important."** And it doesn't stop there. When it comes to offering clear, kind, and consistent feedback, we not only see our team members as people in the present—we're actually seeing the future of a person bursting with possibility. Through believing in and being *transparent* with people, we're actually seeing the person that they've yet to become.

Last but not least, when we lead with the three T's, we *see* people for far more than what they can do for us or the organization. We *see* people as people. People with potential. People with plans. People with families and all sorts of hopes, fears, needs, opportunities, and challenges.

The Keys to Success

When leaders work *together* to make *thoughtful* decisions and lead with *transparency*, we create a culture where people have the very best chance to be *successful*. When we make decisions *together*, we build a foundation for people to achieve better outcomes. More people get to see the beginning, middle, and end of a decision, and with that increased exposure, each team member gets to take what they've learned and carry it into future decisions. In cultures where people make decisions in a vacuum, people learn from their own decisions, but cultures that move *together* learn faster as a unit through walking through a wider array of decisions.

When we make *thoughtful* decisions, we're literally seeing the decisions we make through the lens of others and making choices that set people up for *success*. In lots of organizations, everything is so complex and murky that it's impossible to know when we've won. And yet, when we lead with *transparency*, we provide clarity around vision, strategy, and targets that the whole team is far more likely to embrace and chase. From feedback and directional clarity to things to watch out for, there's nothing quite like *transparency* to set people up for *success*.

"But Josh, what happens when people feel *safe, seen,* and *successful* in their work?"

I'm so glad you asked.

The Keeping It Real sections of this book are full of examples of how people have felt safe and seen, which has led to more success for team members and the company at large. Because when people feel *safe, seen,* and *successful,* they react in extraordinary ways. They dream up new and better approaches to addressing problems and seize opportunities in ways that support the leader, strengthen the team, and spur the We-Cycle on. This is where all the care and intention gets fun and energizing for the leader. It's payoff time!

Level Up

- In considering your team or organization, which of the three (*safe, seen,* and *successful*)
    1. feels most prominent?
    2. seems most elusive?
- Which T would move the needle the most in leading your team to feel more *safe, seen,* and *successful*?
- What's one thing that you can start doing tomorrow to help the people you lead to feel more *safe, seen,* and *successful*?

Keeping It Real

Andy
Video Producer | 1 year at Block

I joined the team just two weeks before the annual retreat. Watching the company set aside time, money, and energy to "sharpen the saw" and bring everyone together was eye-opening. A lot of organizations talk about unity. But Block actually invests in it. That early experience showed me that alignment and culture aren't afterthoughts here; they're priorities.

One thing I really appreciate is the financial transparency. When we're not hitting our targets—whether as a company or individually—it isn't hidden or sugarcoated. We're given the context *early*, not at the eleventh hour. That gives us time to course-correct, which not only helps the business but creates trust in leadership.

There was also a moment when I had to report a situation in which a coworker crossed a serious professional line. I was hesitant, but I went to my manager, and the issue was quickly escalated to our VP and senior leadership. They didn't stall or waver. They took decisive action and kept me in the loop the entire time. By the next day, the issue was resolved. What mattered most was that I was believed, heard, and taken seriously. That told me everything I needed to know about how seriously we protect our culture.

Another time, I was trying something new and could tell it wasn't working. My instinct in past roles would have been to push through anyway, just to say I finished. But here, I felt free to raise my hand and say, "This isn't going to yield what we hoped. Can we scrap it?" And my manager simply said, "Good call. Let's kill it. What's next?" That moment of trust felt incredible.

Block isn't a perfect place, but it's one that *tries*. It puts feet to its promises and constantly works to improve. You're given autonomy, trust, and the space to grow not just professionally, but personally too.

The word that embodies *People Matter at Work* for me is *support*. Support to speak up. Support to try and fail. Support to learn. Support to be taken seriously. And support to become better—at work and in life.

Keeping It Real

Joal

Marketing Communications Specialist | 5 years at Block

One of the first moments *people matter* came alive for me was when Chris Sharrock—someone I didn't know very well at the time—reached out to build a friendship. But it didn't stop there. He also offered to mentor me, simply because he believed I was capable of more. That was the first time someone outside my close circle took a genuine interest in helping me grow, and it left a mark.

Another moment that stands out came early in my time at Block, during a season when I was still finding my place. I was doing good work, but I carried a lot of internal pressure—second-guessing myself and wondering if I was really measuring up. Out of the blue, Chris pulled me aside and said, "You know, I just want you to know you're doing an awesome job. I love what you're creating." He had no way of knowing how much I needed that affirmation. But in that moment, I felt safe, recognized, and confident enough to bring more of myself to the team. It showed me that leadership at Block isn't just focused on output. It's rooted in emotional intelligence and human connection.

There was another time I had spent a lot of effort creating a project for Josh, only to find out it wasn't quite what was needed and had to be scrapped. That kind of thing happens. But instead of brushing past it, Josh paused to acknowledge my work and even apologized for the miscommunication. That moment stood out to me as an example of healthy, humble leadership. It meant more than he probably realized.

Early on, I came in with a mindset shaped by perfectionism and micromanagement. But over time, the trust and support I've received here have helped reshape that. I've grown in emotional maturity, communication, and ownership. I contribute today not just through my creative work but by helping to build a culture of authenticity, collaboration, and growth.

I've realized something important about Block: You can get out of it what you put in. If your goal is just to clock in and out, the culture won't force you to engage. But if you want to grow, learn, and be challenged, you'll find people ready to support and reciprocate that. I've gone from someone who

THE THREE S'S

> second-guessed their value to someone who shows up with confidence, clarity, and care.
>
> The word that sums up *People Matter at Work* for me is *humanity*. Most jobs value you for your output. At Block, you're seen as a person with a life, emotions, and struggles. You're allowed to show up how you are, and you're valued for being human.

CHAPTER 8

Trust

As the three T's came to life in those early years, we began to see the team rowing in the same direction and felt the power of teamwork as our ultimate competitive advantage. While systems and equations can dangerously oversimplify the art of leadership, after more than twenty-five thousand hours of seeking to create a place where people love to work, I'm continually blown away by what happens when leaders work *together* to make *thoughtful* decisions and are *transparent* about what's going on, what the leader's thinking about, and what the leader is thinking about the people they lead. As we've already covered, leading in this way fosters a culture where people feel *safe*, *seen*, and *successful*. And what happens when people feel *safe*, *seen*, and *successful*? I can't wait to share!

The Biggest T of All

Remember me talking about air quality? When it comes to culture and relationships, *trust* is like oxygen—we don't pay much attention when it's there, but we're gasping for air when it's gone. When team members feel *safe*, *seen*, and *successful*, they carry *trust* for their leaders and their organization. When they *don't* feel *safe*, *seen*, and *successful*, they struggle and strain in the absence of trust.

Check out this poignant passage in Stephen Covey's *The Speed of Trust*:

> There is one thing that is common to every individual, relationship, team, family, organization, nation, economy, and civilization throughout the world—one thing which, if removed, will destroy the most powerful government, the most successful business, the most thriving economy, the most influential leadership, the greatest friendship, the strongest character, the deepest love. On the other hand, if developed and leveraged, one thing can create unparalleled success and prosperity in every dimension of life. Yet, it is the least understood, most neglected, and most underestimated possibility of our time. That one thing is trust.[11]

---

[11] Stephen M. R. Covey, *The Speed of Trust: The One Thing That Changes Everything* (New York: Free Press, 2008).

Whoa. Just as Lencioni's ideas on organizational health and teamwork were streetlights on a curvy country road for me, Covey's articulation of the importance of *trust* cuts to the core.

One thing, if removed, will destroy. On the other hand, if developed, trust has the potential to create success and prosperity in every area of life.

Wow, really? Every dimension?

Yet, even with all this power, **it is the least understood, most neglected, and most underestimated possibility of our time.**

Author and business leader Bob Chapman describes his own *trust* conversion in his book *Everybody Matters*:

> I realized much later that my business education had ignored the question of how my leadership would impact the lives of other people; instead, it was how to use people to further my own financial success. I was taught to view people as functions and objects to be used and manipulated to achieve my own goals rather than as full-fledged human beings with hopes, dreams, fears, and aspirations every bit as legitimate as my own.[12]

When we transition from the "me" leadership to a "we" leadership approach that Chapman describes

---

[12] Bob Chapman, *Everybody Matters: The Extraordinary Power of Caring for Your People like Family* (New York: Portfolio, 2015).

above, people's *trust* in our leadership grows. While *trust* isn't the end game, it fuels strong relationships, galvanizes healthy teams, and moves high-performance organizations forward in uncommon ways.

The Power of High-*Trust* Cultures

Here are some incredibly impactful elements of a high-*trust* culture:

- **Low Turnover:** People not only stay but they grow and invest their best.
- **High Efficiency:** *Trust* encourages innovation, risk-taking, and better decision-making.
- **Better Customer Service:** When people feel cared for, it's only natural to turn their attention to care for others—especially customers.
- **Personal Growth:** *Trust* reduces fear and stress, empowering people to metabolize feedback and become the best version of themselves—both at work and at home.
- **Enhanced Performance:** When people *trust* and respect their leaders, they're far more likely to bring creativity, innovation, and passion to their work.

Trust is a game changer. As Dr. Henry Cloud says, "Trust is the currency that drives every relationship."

Trust Is a Two-Way Street

Trust isn't one-directional; it flows both ways. **How you view your team will undoubtedly shape the culture you build.** For better or worse, the leader's perspective and actions serve to create and perpetuate the culture. Oftentimes, people will act in the ways we expect them to. When we see and believe the best in people's potential, we offer opportunities to stretch and grow beyond what even they could have ever imagined. Picture a culture in which your team members become more than they ever dreamed of, such that they actually surprise themselves with what they are able to achieve! And yet, our belief cuts both ways. If we see people as lazy or entitled, we're prone to create a self-fulfilling prophecy and get just that: lazy and entitled team members.

At Block Imaging, we've leaned into initial *trust* by believing in our people's best intentions from the start. Has that *trust* ever been taken advantage of? Of course it has. But the cost of mistrusting everyone would be far greater than the cost of getting burned on rare occasion.

As Covey said, "We tend to get what we expect. When we expect more, we get more." The reality is that in a thriving organization, the cost of someone not bringing their best will have a far greater impact on their own future than on the company's. This causes leaders to challenge people more through the lens of who they're becoming rather than what we can benefit from them at the moment. This little mindset shift changes everything in the way we view and approach the people we lead as well as how they respond with trust or distrust.

Trust in Action: Small Moments, Big Impact

Let's look at two real-world examples of how *trust*—or the lack of it—plays out.

A couple of months ago, I stopped by a sandwich shop where a server made a minor mistake on an order. When the resident sandwich artist recognized the error would require a whole new sandwich, the look of doom came over her face. After setting the half-made sandwich to the side, she went to the back while the customer waited and returned with a clipboard where she feverishly filled out a "sandwich violation report." As she filled out the report, she shared that the "inventory" (slices of meat, cheese, and buns) was audited at the end of every shift.

Standing there, I couldn't help but wonder what this person was thinking and feeling as she filled out this report. Did this policy make her feel more or less *trusted* by her boss? Or maybe she just felt like it was a waste of time and energy when she could have been focusing on getting the customer what they had requested. Don't get me wrong, there's a cost to lost (or stolen) inventory. But it can be easy to forget that there's a cost to *mistrust* too.

In contrast, shortly after this experience, I shopped at a Costco in Sarasota, Florida. At the end of my visit, I paid for the produce and handed my receipt to the receipt checker at the exit doors. Looking down at my cart, I laughed.

"If I was gonna steal something from Costco, it certainly wouldn't be fruit and vegetables," I said.

Before the words had rolled off my tongue, the team member scratched a Sharpie down the middle of the receipt and chuckled back. "Oh, we're not checking to see if you stole something," he said. "We're making sure we didn't double charge you for anything."

Whoa. What did you just say? Talk about a moment. While this was just one situation at one location, I'd bet a forty-count of baked beans that there is a correlation between the sentiment of *trust* Mr. Receipt Checker Guy demonstrated to me that day and Costco being recognized as one of the best workplaces in America. A high-*trust* culture flows through the team and deep into the customer experience.

If Walls Could Talk

Let's take a moment to assess where we are on the *trust* spectrum. None of us will have full visibility or perfect *trust* with every person and in every situation. But as I shared earlier, our teams have a keen sense of what's important to us and whether we really care about them deep down. Not generically, hypothetically, or occasionally, but tangibly, authentically, specifically, and consistently.

If you're a leader doing this really well, I'd bet a Heath-and-salted-caramel concrete mixer from Culver's that if I spent just fifteen minutes with your team, I'd feel it. There would be relational warmth and laughter, ease in the way people communicate and work *together*, and a team with a lot of freedom to shape ideas, make things better, and take great care of customers and team members alike.

I'm still amazed at the surprise and affirmation that comes from taking people on a tour of our headquarters. Sometimes people make a comment about the café in the front corridor or the greeting card stations placed here and there for team members to recognize one another's joys, sorrows, and success. Other times it's how we greet so many people by name or the team's reaction as we pass by. I can't tell you the number of times people have commented on people's ease as "the executives" move through their space. For every guest who says how impressed they were that people stopped their work to warmly greet us, there's another guest who comments about the fact that people were having a casual conversation about NASCAR and didn't scatter back to their desks when senior leaders showed up. Those are just a few examples of what you might see in an environment where leaders trust their people and that trust is reciprocated.

Just the Beginning

Trust is the first of three "We-Actions" that flow out of a culture where people feel *safe*, *seen*, and *successful*. Now that we've got the We-Cycle spinning, there are two final elements that will spur an organization forward in ways that once seemed unimaginable.

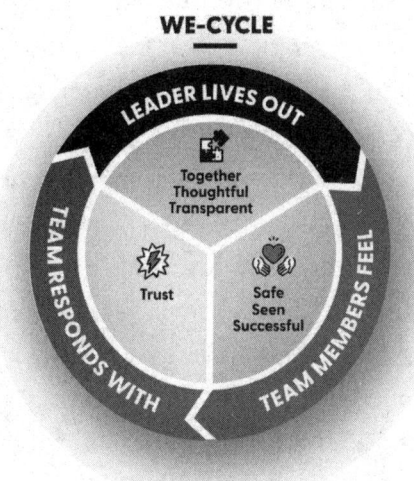

Level Up

- Why do you think the level of (high or low) *trust* in your team is where it is today?
- If the people you lead could hear every conversation and see every email, would their *trust* in your leadership grow or shrink?
- Which T (*together*, *thoughtful*, or *transparent*) would serve to grow *trust* in your team the most?

Keeping It Real

Eric

Parts Return Manager | 2 years at Block

People matter was a value I held long before joining Block. But once I became part of the team, hearing those words spoken day after day, week after week opened my eyes to how often that value is *lived out* here. It's in the small things, the everyday interactions, the way people treat each other.

I've seen the three T's—*together, thoughtful,* and *transparent*—on display often. Thankfully, tough conversations are rare, but when they do happen, there's always a shared desire to work through them with respect. The goal isn't just to resolve a conflict; it's to honor each other in the process.

One place I experience that most consistently is in my 1:1s with my leader. I actually *look forward* to those meetings. She's incredible at creating a safe space where I feel seen and heard. I'm challenged, supported, and given the tools I need to succeed. That kind of intentional leadership creates real growth.

Another moment that stands out is how we care for each other in life transitions—like when someone's family is growing. The way people rally to provide gifts and support speaks volumes. It's a reflection of who we are as a team.

Since joining Block, one of the biggest areas I've grown in is confidence. The work we do isn't easy, but the culture of transparency gave me permission to ask questions and lean into challenges. I knew I'd be met with encouragement, not judgment. That's how growth happens here.

If someone asked me what makes Block different, I'd say this: It's a place where your value as a *person* comes before your productivity. *People Matter at Work* is best summed up in one word: *honor*. Every person I work with has inherent value, and when I choose to honor them for that, it changes how I communicate, how I lead, and how I show up. That's the culture we're building, and it makes all the difference.

CHAPTER 9

Ownership and Generosity

Last but not least, when people feel *safe*, *seen*, and *successful*, they not only *trust* but they respond by taking *ownership*.

Drive It like You Own It!

If you'll humor me for a moment, I'd like to share how this book came to be. Believe it or not, it took nearly six years to get this book completed from start to finish. After being asked repeatedly when I would compile these stories and principles into book form, in the fall of 2019 I felt the nudge to get it started when I was out for a run. In May of 2020, with the world at a bit of a standstill, our children not in school, and most of the company working remotely, our family rented a cabin in Gatlinburg, Tennessee, with the purpose of starting the writing process. I wrote and wrote and wrote. Fast-forward to 2021; having trouble carving out time, I hired an editor, hoping to regain momentum.

From 2021 to 2023, Block Imaging was in the midst of being acquired by a joint venture comprising two extraordinary organizations: Siemens Healthineers and CommonSpirit Health. To anyone who has ever been involved in an acquisition, it won't be surprising to hear that the book again took a back seat. Over the next eighteen months, as Block doubled in size, while new stories and situations served to deepen my belief in what we were practicing and experiencing, finding time to carry the book to the finish line was tough.

As 2024 rolled around, I knew it was time. It had been five years since that initial nudge to write, and my deep passion for seeing leaders create cultures where people thrive and everyone wins had grown stronger than ever. In hopes of getting *People Matter at Work* into the end zone, I made a list and reached out to the grittiest and most tenacious people I knew for help.

OWNERSHIP AND GENEROSITY

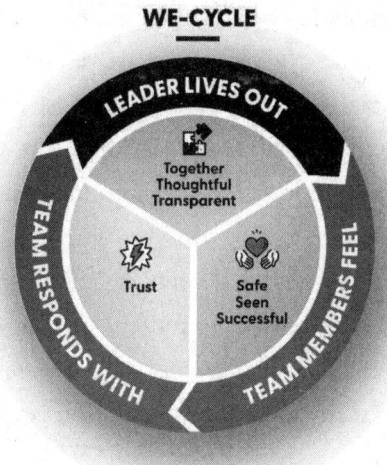

Thankfully, my friend Andy said yes and dove headlong into Block Imaging and the writing process. He attended our all-team meetings for a season, and as part of the editorial process, he asked if he could interview a dozen team members from all over the organization. I said sure and worked with our leadership team to select a broad array of team members with all sorts of different roles and tenures with the company that ranged from six months to twenty years.

I share all this background because it took an outside observer like Andy to highlight a key piece of the We-Cycle and how people respond when they feel *safe*, *seen*, and *successful*.

Andy remarked one day, "Josh, the one thing that I notice that's head and shoulders above any other organization I've worked with is the deep sense of *ownership* that people carry here. Over and over again, they speak about the organization like it belongs to them."

To be entirely honest, this was equal parts an aha moment and something I'd just taken for granted. In leading and working with hundreds of people over the years, I'd felt that shared sense of *ownership* from so many on our team for so long that I didn't even think to articulate it as an essential part of the We-Cycle.

I love how Jocko Willink speaks about leadership and *ownership* in *Extreme Ownership*: "As a leader, if you are down in the weeds planning the details with your guys, you will have the same perspective as them, which adds little value. But if you let them plan the details, it allows them to own their piece of the plan."[13] This was one of those moments for me.

Owning vs. Renting

If you've ever been on either end of buying, selling, or renting a house or apartment, you'll know the difference between how owners and tenants treat houses, cars, or

---

[13] Jocko Willink and Leif Babin, *Extreme Ownership: How U.S. Navy SEALs Lead and Win* (New York: St. Martin's Press, 2015).

companies. Ever changed the roof on an apartment you were renting? Ever put premium gas in or vacuumed out a rental car? *Merriam-Webster* defines *ownership* as "the quality or state of being accountable." Another word that fits in well with *ownership* and *accountability* is *responsibility*. Without belaboring the point, someone who's responsible is *trustworthy* and able to answer for their attitudes and actions.

People with a sense of *ownership* want what's best for their organization. **People who carry *ownership* bring their best, take risks, speak up, grow up, solve problems, seize opportunities, serve customers, and think in ways that those who don't carry *ownership* won't.** This is a game changer for leaders and organizations at large. People who carry an owner's mindset are far more likely to look out for their leader's *success* and well-being as well as focus on the long-term *success* and well-being of the company.

Ownership is a self-perpetuating turbine powered by reciprocal *trust* and honor: The leader values the team, the team values the organization, everybody grows, and everybody wins. Check out how far we've come in exploring the We-Cycle now that we've dug into the power of *trust* and *ownership*.

WE-CYCLE

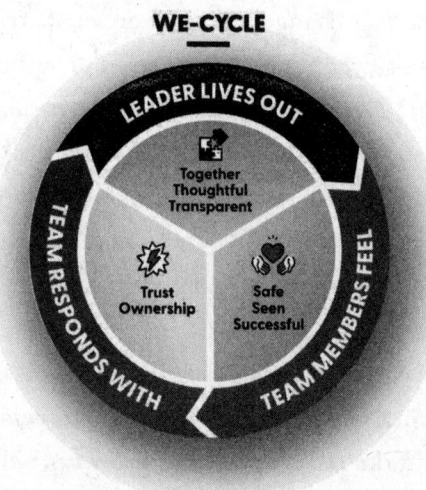

The Grand Finale: *Generosity*

Hold on tight, because this is where the magic really happens. When people feel *safe*, *seen*, and *successful*, they not only carry deep *trust* and a sense of *ownership* for the organization but they give back *generously* to the leaders and organization that have given generously to them. *Merriam-Webster* speaks to *generosity* in three distinct ways. It is

1. liberal in giving, open-handed;
2. marked by abundance or ample portions, copious; and
3. characterized by a noble or kindly spirit, magnanimous.

Does that describe the organization you're a part of or the people you lead? If so, that's a great sign that you're on the right track. If that feels like a million miles from reality, that just means we have some work to do.

One of the biggest frustrations I hear from leaders as they speak about their teams—and in particular the newest generation of the workforce—is a sense of entitlement. **A sense of entitlement is unattractive and counterproductive, but it's also a preemptive defense against a system that an employee assumes will exploit or treat them poorly.** When we embody the three T's, we build *trust* and deepen *ownership* such that entitlement has nowhere to gain and generosity takes its place.

Reciprocating Safety: Protecting the Organization

In a Me-Cycle culture, employees focus primarily on protecting themselves, with risk mitigation and security resting in a few designated roles. In contrast, a We-Cycle culture makes protection a shared responsibility. When people feel *safe* at work, they're far more likely to go out of their way to protect the organization they love. Here, everyone is encouraged to proactively identify risks and protect the organization, each carrying a deep sense of *ownership* and accountability for the company's well-being.

This responsibility extends beyond mere compliance; it's a collective duty of care. Team members look out for each other and the organization, acting as advocates for their leaders, teammates, and the mission.

One example is how team members recruit and endorse candidates they think should join the team. When people love where they work, they're naturally inclined to invite people they respect to invest in and protect the organization. When a team member who carries *ownership* and knows what we value endorses a candidate, it's a huge vote of confidence. At the same time, if their experience with the person raises a caution flag, they also protect the company by filtering out individuals who may not be a good fit from a character, chemistry, or competence perspective.

From navigating a difficult customer situation to catching a mistake on a contract to holding the team accountable or moving a CT scanner safely, there are countless ways for people to protect the organization. This sense of mutual care not only safeguards the organization but also enhances its resilience. *Together*, team members become more attuned to potential issues and feel empowered to address them as a unified team.

In a We-Cycle culture in which people embody *ownership* and reciprocate by ensuring safety, protection isn't just another task; it's recognized as essential

to preserving the environment we've collectively built. Over time, this protection becomes a defining strength of the organization, laying a solid foundation for its long-term stability and *success*.

Giving Back During COVID

Our investment in looking out for people first has paid off in countless ways. Little did we know, a few weeks into the pandemic the government would begin providing strong unemployment incentives that would set up a portion of our team to earn more to stay home than to show up for work. Instead of sitting back and collecting unemployment checks until they were forced to come back, our team showed up repeatedly as they sought to extend *generosity* to the leaders and company that first looked out for them. Born out of feeling *safe*, the team protected the company in this incredibly difficult time.

After years of working *together* to make *thoughtful* decisions and lead with *transparency*, the We-Cycle was spinning at full force. As weeks turned into months, we resumed chasing our targets again. With some businesses propped up and others handcuffed by supply-chain issues, we hit our financial markers in 2020 and grew the business by 25 percent in 2021.

Seeing and Responding to the Organization's Needs

Walking in *generosity* is about so much more than safety and protection. When people are *seen* and invested in as people, they're far more likely to *see* and invest in the needs of the business on a deeper level. Most of our team has worked somewhere else. I love hearing each new team member share in Block University what they've noticed about our culture since joining. Some share about the hiring process while others talk about the warm welcome. One of my favorites is how helpful and accessible everyone is as the new team members are getting acclimated. They can immediately feel the difference in being a part of this team.

In healthy cultures, people are acutely aware of what the organization offers them. The more leaders carefully consider the needs of their people, the more people are likely to take careful consideration of the needs of the organization. When people's needs have been tended to, they shift their focus from simply completing tasks and surviving another day to dreaming up and diving into initiatives that align with the long-term vision of the organization.

The opportunities for team members to see the needs of the business are endless. From seizing opportunities to finding solutions or acting on potential improvements, it's incredible to see what happens when people's focus shifts from primarily looking out for themselves to being part of something bigger. Just like with protecting the organization, strategy no longer falls to one person or department; it becomes a team sport.

When we lead followers, we focus on tasks. When we lead leaders, we focus on vision and direction; the team in turn focuses on the approach and tasks necessary to accomplish initiatives. Team members who look out for the organization's needs don't need to be tasked or prompted, because they already carry *trust* and *ownership*. They bring a sense of ownership, going above and beyond what's required because they feel genuinely connected to the organization's *success*. It's their success too. Whether it's noticing an inefficiency in a process and recommending a way to streamline it or volunteering to fill gaps or take on additional responsibilities, people whose needs are *seen* will go out of their way to *see* and *see to* the needs around them.

When leaders create a culture in which people feel *seen*, it paves the way for a team to be engaged and invested in the organization's ongoing improvement. This willingness to see and address the organization's needs transforms everyday tasks into meaningful contributions to the organization's future. After all, people who carry *trust* for the leaders and a deep sense of *ownership* know that when the team fails, they fail, and when the organization succeeds, they succeed.

In Pursuit of Enduring *Success*

When we as leaders are *transparent* about mission and vision, how the company is performing, and the ways each team member can grow and make an impact, then people and teams come *together* powerfully to do incredible things to drive the organization forward.

When people feel *successful* and empowered in their roles, they begin to see the organization's achievements as their own. This perspective shift is central to the We-Cycle: Team members don't just work for personal *success*; they work to uplift the entire organization. *Generosity* becomes a multiplier with each contribution inspiring further contributions across the team.

A culture that celebrates individual and team achievements fosters a natural desire in people to contribute to the organization's collective *success*. From knowledge-sharing and mentorship to stepping in during a critical project or providing support to a teammate in need, healthy companies are filled with helpful people. In this environment, *success* is a shared accomplishment. People want to support others, knowing that each person's growth contributes to the whole. They're motivated to lift up their colleagues and help the organization reach new heights, understanding that the group's *success* reflects positively on everyone involved.

And That's How It's Done

In 2023, my brother Jeremy had what's called a "widow-maker" heart attack at age forty-five. Just days after a new hospital's grand opening, he was the first patient to undergo an interventional procedure there. Having provided all manner of radiology equipment to healthcare providers around the world, it was a pretty humbling experience. Jeremy came out okay, but given his close call and our family history of heart disease, I decided to get checked out by a cardiologist and ultimately undergo a CT angiogram exam. Shortly after the scan was read, the doctor shared that while heart disease wasn't an issue, it appeared that I had an aortic aneurysm in my abdomen.

After an abdominal CT, I was referred to the University of Michigan and scheduled for surgery on December 23, 2023. I was told ahead of time that there was a 50/50 shot as to whether I'd undergo surgery that morning or wait until after the holidays, but when we arrived, someone looked at my scan and proceeded like it was a given. Lacey and I were told repeatedly how fortunate we were to have found the aneurysm as most don't make it to the hospital in time in the case of a rupture.

Within minutes, the nurse was asking me what music I'd like to listen to as they slid me onto the angio table. Over the next three hours, the surgeon and several others worked *together* to treat the aneurysm. Mostly awake to the conversation so that I could hold my breath at the proper times, I could tell that they were struggling to gain access to the space they were looking to glue off. Several physicians had attempted, but none were able to navigate the winding path to success. Just when I heard them discussing whether to step back and move on to a more invasive surgery, one of the surgeons remarked, "And that's how it's done!!"

Looking back, I'm so grateful for the team's effort and the surgeon's one last effort to *successfully* arrive at and seal off the weakened vessel. Though they perform countless surgeries together every year, I'm so grateful for their training and tenacity in successfully completing the procedure that day.

Likewise, in a vibrant We-Cycle, *trust*, *ownership*, and *generosity* become more than just behaviors—they become part of an organization's identity and character. And when people carry *trust*, *ownership*, and *generosity*, everyone wins. While in some ways *generosity* is the end, it comes back around to energize leaders and keep the We-Cycle spinning. Over time, the load gets lighter for leaders, more fulfilling for team members, more effectual for customers, and more enriching for families and every person the organization encounters.

And that's how it's done.

Level Up

- Is the sense of *ownership* and *generosity* among your team high or low?
- Why do you think it is at the level it is right now?
- If you could snap your fingers and increase *trust*, *ownership*, or *generosity*, which would it be and why?
- What's the next step to close the gap between where you are and where you hope to be in twelve months?

Keeping It Real

Zack

Service Coordinator | 2 years at Block

People matter came alive for me almost immediately after joining Block. I was still grieving the sudden loss of my brother. He passed away the same day I interviewed. Starting a new job while carrying that weight felt overwhelming. But from day one, my team met me with compassion, patience, and genuine care. Rather than adding to my stress, the workplace became a source of healing.

One moment that sticks with me happened the day before the anniversary of my brother's passing. I told Kelsey, our receptionist, how I was feeling, and she immediately stepped in and comforted me, spoke to my manager, and encouraged me to take the time I needed. Shortly after, my leader gave me a hug and told me to take the next two days off—no PTO required. That simple gesture made a lasting impact. I didn't just feel supported; I felt safe and seen.

I was proud to be part of the Block team in those moments when support showed up not just in words but in action. From stepping in when I needed a break to showing up for my family, the people around me lived out *people matter* in real, tangible ways.

Since joining Block, I've grown in resilience and gratitude. Being in a place where people genuinely care has helped me find strength I didn't know I had. I've learned to work under pressure, collaborate closely with others, and stay present even in difficult seasons.

Block Imaging is more than a workplace—it's a community. Block has cared for me as a whole person, not just what I can produce. Here, people don't just acknowledge your struggles; they *walk with you* through them. And that has made all the difference in one of the hardest chapters of my life.

CONCLUSION

The Ripple Effect of *People Matter* Leadership

As we come to the end of this journey *together*, I want to leave you with two of my favorite vision-casting words: *What if?* They serve to unlock our imagination, fire up our prefrontal cortex, and help us envision a richly imagined future.

So let me ask:

What if more leaders led with the We-Cycle at the forefront?

What if *your* organization did?

What would happen to the people who work there? To the customers you serve? The vendors you partner with? The marriages and friendships of the people you lead and the communities they're a part of? Or what about the children that the people you lead come home to at the end of every day?

How might their view of work—and even their view of the world—begin to shift?

Less fear. More joy.

Less loneliness. More connection.

Less dread. More fulfillment.

This is what's possible when we lead in a way that puts people first. And it starts with leaders like you.

Some of us deeply want to be leaders worth following. I hope that's you. And if it is, I want you to know: I see you, and I'm for you. Whether you feel too busy, too uncertain, or just a little stuck, you're not alone in this journey.

It feels like just yesterday I was twenty-nine years old, staring at the ceiling, wondering how to take the first step up what felt like a daunting mountain. A decade and a half later, I've learned more than I ever imagined and yet my advice to myself then, and to you now, is borrowed from my dear friend Katie Davis Majors, who founded the remarkable Amazima School in Jinja, Uganda:

Just take the next right step.

Whether it's dreaming about the future, hiring an incredible assistant, having that high-stakes conversation, apologizing for missed marks, launching something new, paying down debt, or reshaping the culture, ask yourself: *What does taking the next right step look like?*

To underscore the entire message of this book: Where we place our focus as leaders matters deeply.

CONCLUSION

One of my favorite leadership pictures comes from a quote that's attributed to Lao Tzu:

> Go to the people.
> Live with them.
> Learn from them.
> Love them.
> Start with what they know.
> Build on what they have.
> But with the best leaders,
> when the work is done,
> the task accomplished,
> the people will say,
> "We have done it ourselves."

This is the kind of leadership that changes workplaces and lives.

So, here's to you.

To the leader you're becoming.

To the people you're serving.

To the ripple effect you're creating.

Let's keep asking "what if"—and then go find out, *together*.

If I can serve you in fostering a place where people love to work, say the word. It would be my privilege to support you on the journey. You can contact me at:

josh@peoplematteratwork.com

Further Reading

Huge thanks to the authors who've helped shape my life and leadership. You've made me look way smarter than I am and have had an enormous influence on my life. *Together* we've helped create a place where so many people love to work.

Arbinger Institute, *Leadership and Self-Deception: Getting Out of the Box* (Oakland, California: Berrett-Koehler, 2016)

Brené Brown, *Dare to Lead: Brave Work. Tough Conversations. Whole Hearts.* (New York: Random House, 2018)

Jim Collins and Morten T. Hansen, *Great by Choice: Uncertainty, Chaos, and Luck—Why Some Thrive Despite Them All* (New York: Harper Business, 2011)

"The Greatest Showman, Featurette—Hugh Jackman, 2017," posted December 20, 2017, by 20th Century Studios Danmark, YouTube, https://www.youtube.com/watch?v=6-CCxYR80mU

FURTHER READING

Eric Greitens, *Resilience: Hard-Won Wisdom for Living a Better Life* (New York: Harvest, 2016)

Chip Heath and Dan Heath, *The Power of Moments: Why Certain Experiences Have Extraordinary Impact* (New York: Simon & Schuster, 2017)

James M. Kouzes and Barry Z. Posner, *The Leadership Challenge: How to Make Extraordinary Things Happen in Organizations, Seventh Edition* (Hoboken, New Jersey: John Wiley & Sons, 2023)

Patrick M. Lencioni, *The Advantage: Why Organizational Health Trumps Everything Else in Business* (London: Jossey-Bass, 2011)

Patrick M. Lencioni, *The Five Dysfunctions of a Team: A Leadership Fable* (London: Jossey-Bass, 2002)

John Maxwell, *The 21 Irrefutable Laws of Leadership: Follow Them and People Will Follow You* (Nashville: Thomas Nelson, 1998)

Andy Stanley, *Next Generation Leader: 5 Essentials for Those Who Will Shape the Future* (Colorado Springs, Colorado: Multnomah, 2006)

Benjamin Zander, "Life Lessons from Beethoven's Symphony No. 9," TED Talk, Vancouver, BC, April 2023, 19 min., 13 sec., https://www.ted.com/talks/benjamin_zander_life_lessons_from_beethoven_s_symphony_no_9

Chris Zook and James Allen, *The Founder's Mentality: How to Overcome the Predictable Crises of Growth* (Boston: Harvard Business Review Press, 2016)